Victoria Cross

from ♡

W9-BJB-034

Medd 1967

Victoria Cross

from

Medd 1967

NORTH AMERICAN BIRDS

Other books illustrated by Marie Nonnast Bohlen

Amikuk by Rutherford Montgomery
Seloe by Betty John
White Tail by Rutherford Montgomery
Graywings by Alice Gondey
Red Legs by Alice Gondey
My Ladybug by Wong-Vessel
Wild Swans and Geese by Edwin Mason
The Random House Encyclopedia of Natural History

Other books by Lorus and Margery Milne

The Nature of Animals
The Phoenix Forest
The Ages of Life
Patterns of Survival
Living Plants of the World
Gift from the Sky
The Crab That Crawled Out of the Past
Water and Life
Because of a Tree
The Valley: Meadow, Grove and Stream
The Senses of Animals and Men
The Mountains [with the Editors of Life]
The Balance of Nature
The Lower Animals [with Ralph and Mildred Buchsbaum]
Plant Life
Animal Life
Paths Across the Earth
The World of Night
The Mating Instinct
The Biotic World and Man
Famous Naturalists
A Multitude of Living Things

NORTH AMERICAN BIRDS

By Lorus and Margery Milne

Paintings by Marie Nonnast Bohlen

PRENTICE-HALL, INC. ENGLEWOOD CLIFFS, NEW JERSEY

NORTH AMERICAN BIRDS by Lorus and Margery Milne   Illustrated by Marie Nonnast
Bohlen   Text © 1969 by Prentice-Hall, Inc.   Illustrations © 1963, 1969 by Fawcett
Publications   Copyright under International and Pan American Copyright Conventions
13-623769-X   All rights reserved. No part of this book may be reproduced in any form or
by any means, except for the inclusion of brief quotations in a review, without permission
in writing from the publisher. Library of Congress Catalog Card Number: 7 5 - 8 5 4 0 4
Printed in the United States of America. T   Prentice-Hall International, Inc., London
Prentice-Hall of Australia, Pty. Ltd., Sydney   Prentice-Hall of Canada, Ltd., Toronto
Prentice-Hall of India Private Ltd., New Delhi   Prentice-Hall of Japan, Inc., Tokyo

CONTENTS

For *Oliver Payne Pearson* and *Anita Kelley Pearson,*
who have ranged far in vertebrate zoology since growing up near
Pennsylvania's Perkiomen Creek where Audubon pioneered in banding birds,
and for *Carol, Peter, Sandy* and *Alison,*
who helped their parents tag animals while growing close to nature
on the golden hills of California

LIST OF ILLUSTRATIONS

NORTH AMERICAN BIRDS

INTRODUCTION

LESS THAN FOUR CENTURIES HAVE PASSED SINCE THE FIRST DESCRIPTIONS AND illustrations of North American birds appeared in print. These words and pictures were the work of English naturalists who accompanied the second expedition (1584–1585) sent to the "new found land of Virginia" by Sir Walter Raleigh. Thomas Hariot included in his report "to the investors, well-wishers, and friends of the settling and planting of Virginia" a paragraph concerning birds:

> *Turkey cocks* and *turkey hens, stockdoves, partridges, cranes,* and *herons. Swans* and *geese,* which could be had in winter in great abundance, may be added to these. I have noted in the native language the names of eighty-six different kinds of fowl. Besides those I have already named, we have caught and eaten, as well as made pictures of, several different varieties of waterfowl and seventeen kinds of land fowl. We have seen and eaten many others as well, but had not the leisure to draw pictures of them. . . . We found also *parrots, falcons,* and *merlins,* which we do not use for food, but I thought it would be well to mention them for other reasons.

These comments, along with engravings from the watercolors of John White, were published in London in 1588 and 1590 as the observations of men already well versed in the natural history of

North American Birds

Britain. White's original drawings are preserved in the British Museum, and show the head of a brown pelican (the "alcatrassa"), a noddy tern (the "tinosa"), an immature brown booby (the "bobo"), a magnificent frigatebird, and a tropicbird.

Reflecting on these notes, made along the present middle-Atlantic states, we realize that all of the birds pictured were at the northern limit of their modern ranges. By contrast, the swans and geese mentioned would have been whistling swans, Canada geese, snow geese, and brant, all south for the winter to tidewater from homes in the Far North.

The presence of turkey cocks and hens must have been more astonishing to Hariot than his words suggest. He surely knew that domesticated birds of this kind had been introduced into England only in 1541, as the descendants of strange and useful living trophies the Spanish conquistadores had brought back from their exploits in Mexico. Yet here in forested country (now a part of North Carolina) were the same large edible birds roaming wild. No wonder Hariot listed them first, and doubled the impact of his news by mentioning both sexes!

For about a century and a half, North America remained too primitive, too lacking in roads and regular transport for anyone to think of its wildlife as a whole. The English traveler Mark Catesby tried to describe and illustrate some of the denizens he encountered in the New World, presenting them in a two-volume treatise entitled *Natural History of Carolina, Florida and the Bahama Islands.* Published in London in 1754, it seems to have been more of a reference book to acquaint prospective American colonists with what they could expect to see and experience upon their arrival. Only the more obvious animals, plants, and geological features are included.

Alexander Wilson, a Scotsman who emigrated to America in 1794 with only a gun and the clothes on his back, became the pioneer bird artist and writer. Between 1808 and his death in 1813, seven illustrated volumes of his *American Ornithology* appeared. Two additional books, published posthumously, fulfilled the promise made to subscribers for the set. Today it is hard to realize the difficulties under which this determined naturalist managed to earn his precarious living, explore for birds, illustrate and write, supervise publication of each volume and the hand-coloring of the plates, and also solicit subscriptions from possible patrons at the then formidable price of $100 for nine volumes.

Among those Wilson approached with a sample copy in hand was John James Audubon, a man nineteen years younger yet already skilled in painting bird portraits from live or freshly killed specimens, portrayed in natural settings. The stiff illustrations of stuffed birds in Wilson's book offended Audubon, who knew how much better they might have been executed. But a few years later, when Audubon took a portfolio of his own fine work to Philadelphia to seek a publisher in the city that then was the cultural capital of America, he found supporters of Wilson's work intolerant of any competition. Not until 1827 (and then in London) was he able to get his own *Birds of America* beyond the stage of a dream, and his spectacular collection of drawings into production. Then Audubon too became a dedicated traveler, hunter, painter, publisher, and solicitor of subscriptions. His achievement still seems incredible—400 plates, all with the birds drawn life-sized, at $1000 per set. The program expanded as it went along, until in 1838 when he finished, there were 435 plates, all from copper engravings produced in England and hand-colored to his satisfaction. To provide space for the biggest bird Audubon had met—the American turkey—the whole work was in "elephant folio" size. (Elephant folio is at least 36 inches tall.)

To help his subscribers visualize each specimen as a living creature, Audubon wrote an accompanying *Ornithological Biography* in five volumes. He described his own experiences with each species he illustrated, gave measurements—even the weights of eggs—and a wealth of detail on calls, nesting habits, behavior, food, range and place in the natural scheme. His vivid accounts outshone those of Wilson, although both men provided an irreplaceable picture of American birds before deforestation and market hunting decimated the continent's wildlife.*

The need for a less expensive examination of American ornithology was filled in Audubon's time by a well-traveled Yorkshire naturalist, Thomas Nuttall, who served at Harvard University from 1825 to 1834 as lecturer on natural history and curator of the botanic garden. Nuttall's *Manual of the Ornithology of the United States and Canada* appeared in many editions, the last in 1903. His name

* Not until a century later did anyone provide a more complete account of so many North American birds. A textile manufacturer in Massachusetts, Arthur Cleveland Bent, undertook to combine his own field observations into a 22-volume series sponsored by the Smithsonian Institution, as *Life Histories of North American Birds*. Within the past decade, this great work has been reprinted, unchanged, in a paperback edition, at just over $55 for the set.

was honored in the Nuttall Ornithological Club founded in Massachusetts in 1873, an association that enlarged ten years later to become the principal organization of professional ornithologists in the New World—the American Ornithologists' Union, known widely by its initials as the A. O. U. Its technical journal, *Auk,* and its official *Check-list of North American Birds* are standard reference. Members of the A. O. U. interested in the more popular aspects of bird study established the separate National Audubon Society in 1905, which has since become a strong force in modern conservation activities. The Society, with many branches, publishes an attractive illustrated *Audubon Magazine* and also owns many sanctuaries for wildlife, managing still others that are locally held.

Alexander Wilson has not been forgotten. A Wilson Ornithological Society was organized in 1888; it continues to publish *The Wilson Bulletin* on North American birds and to hold annual meetings where recent discoveries are made known to enthusiastic birders.

The invention of photography and improvements in both cameras and films have added new ways to record birds' colorful patterns and activities for those who are unable to make prolonged field studies. Sound-recording and playback equipment enable still more to become familiar with living birds even before meeting them out of doors. But the camera cannot separate the wild bird from the bush, nor the tape recorder distinguish bird song from background noise. The artist's skill makes good the lack of natural emphasis by providing just the details that help us know the bird by its color, shape, and action.

The artist has a choice and reflects personal preference in his decisions. His emphasis can go to feather patterns, ignoring the natural highlights and shadows of the three-dimensional bird in sunlight. This was the preference of Louis Agassiz Fuertes. Or the details can be played down in favor of the general form, shown with the colors as they are in nature—modified by the filtering of sunlight through green leaves or the reflection of sun from the brown of the forest floor. Frank Weston Benson took this approach. Or the bird can become a stylized diagram, seen from conventional angles and isolated in a field of white or gray, to emphasize features one should look for in distinguishing one kind from another. Roger Tory Peterson has made special contributions in this technique. Still other artists, having watched live birds for countless hours, feel that some high moment—like one flash of a motion picture film upon the screen—captures the essence of their feathered being. Marie Nonnast Bohlen paints North American birds in this style, so like that of Audubon. To do so, she has gone to meet her models in their many different habitats.

So our book travels around the continent, from sea coast to mountain peak, from city park to open plain, from lake and river to desert, from the Rio Grande and Florida Keys far toward the North Pole. In it we meet about half—the best known—of the different kinds of birds that nest in this continental area and its offshore islands. We won't see all the birds of North America. But few indeed are the dedicated birders who during a lifetime have seen the more than 600 species living on our continent.

CHAPTER ONE

THE GREAT MIGRATIONS

IN NORTH AMERICA, ONE OUT OF EVERY TWENTY PEOPLE IS A BIRD-WATCHER. Of these birders, more than 10 million increase their pleasures by keeping detailed lists of what they see. Some keep a sort of running inventory, a life list, in which are tallied the date and place and circumstances when each kind of bird was identified in the field for the first time. Many compare every year with the preceding seasons to see whether the migrant birds are early or late, the neighborhood birds few or many. To us, it is both gratifying and slightly incredible that so many feathered inhabitants can be seen or heard through the windows of a suburban house. In the past decade our own recorded list has grown from 30 to 76 kinds, mostly since the trees and shrubs planted around our home have enlarged and since more birds find their way to the feeding trays and water bath we fill.

Just this morning we noticed a pair of catbirds on the ground under our honeysuckle bush. One was leading, the other pursuing, but at a friendly, gentle pace. The leader made no attempt to get more than fifteen inches ahead, and the pursuer never quite caught up. All the time this courtship chase continued, the two catbirds pretended to be just looking for edible insects and worms—but with-

7

out eating anything. If these were the same catbirds that have nested in our spruce trees every summer, then this year, according to our list, they were earlier than average—May 5 in a range from May 2 to 19. But all the other signs of spring have been earlier too: the redwing blackbirds in the marsh, the marsh marigolds and dandelions in flower. We wondered how the catbirds judge the season, to what cue they respond in timing their arrival. Their early appearance might mean that they traveled fewer miles toward Florida while our blustery winter came and went. Or some sign may have started them northward sooner, or good weather might have let them make the full trip in faster time.

We could not be sure that both birds had arrived together, as companions in migration. Our honeysuckle bush could be the site of a rendezvous they keep each May. The leading bird might choose the bush year after year, and wait for whatever mate stopped long enough to raise a family.

For seven years a pair of white-eyed iridescent grackles has nested in our spruces. Six times they have chosen the same tree along the driveway. Once, bothered by workmen, they compromised and accepted another spruce so as to be farthest from the noise and commotion.

Recovery of banded, numbered birds has shown that all common grackles, including those we see, go early each autumn to the southeastern United States. Arriving with us in March, variously on the 18th, the 12th, the 15th, the 24th, the 28th, and the 20th, these two still manage to get their first brood of squawking, short-tailed, brown-eyed youngsters airborne before mid-May. They drive away all other grackles, including their own young, as soon as each can be independent. This leaves the parents free to nest again and produce a second brood.

While the parent grackles are on guard, no other bird of any kind is tolerated in the nest tree. Even the next treetop is taboo to the male song sparrow, who arrives in late March or early April to stake out a domain. Beyond that distance, the grackles ignore him while he lifts his beak and voice, puffs out his chest, and displays the rows of dark streaks and the central brown spot on it, identifying himself vocally and visually. He will welcome a mate who will build him a nest in the shrubbery, but whatever site she chooses becomes forbidden territory to any other sparrow-sized bird.

By June the land around our home is divided up firmly among house wrens, tree swallows, robins, and chipping sparrows. Before the first of July the whole continent is similarly subdivided among an estimated 20 billion birds. Those birds that are too young, or unsuited in some other way, flit between the territories of established birds or flock together for mutual defense. Often they are more conspicuous than the females of mated pairs, who generally blend with the nest site and so contribute to the safety of the young.

Schedules among the different kinds of birds in each area have evolved in ways that reduce competition. Some parents are incubating while others are hunting intensively for live insects of specific sizes. The busy wrens start off their new-hatched chicks with really tiny flies. The robins bring larger food to their young of the same age. As the chicks grow and their appetites enlarge even faster than their gaping mouths, the parents gather more as well as bigger insects.

During those months people most enjoy being outdoors, the nestlings are most numerous and the parents so busy bringing food that some of their natural wariness disappears. North America is then a good place to look for birds. It has more than 20 per cent of the world's feathered creatures concentrated on less than 17 per cent of the planet's land area.

Still, there are great differences in the amount of privacy each kind of bird requires. Some, such as the chipping sparrows that nest in the clipped shrubbery beside our front walk, stay perfectly still while people walk within arm's reach. If we stand quietly at the same distance, we can watch them fly into the bush from the far side and feed their nestlings in plain sight.

At the opposite extreme (and with good reason) most birds of prey are so fearful of any human presence near their nests that they will let their young starve rather than approach while people remain in the vicinity. To view these birds without being a disturbance, an observer needs a hiding place. An elaborate observation post of this kind was built in Scotland, near Speyside, to let British naturalists see, through twenty-power binoculars, the only remaining nest of ospreys in the United Kingdom. It would be a pity if North Americans allowed their timid birds to similarly dwindle by intrusion, by too great an invasion of their privacy.

Just as among newborn mammals, newhatched birds vary tremendously in the length of time they must be cared for in the nest. Baby

North American Birds

hummingbirds appear as naked and premature as young rats, whereas a baby quail is ready to dry itself off and follow its parent. Young plovers hatched on a sea beach and young whippoorwills emerging from the egg shell in equally simple nests on the forest floor are almost impossible to find because they move off quickly and wear perfect camouflage. Perhaps their parents do not always find them to give them food—another of the natural hazards that limits reproductive success.

Despite the often fatal interest taken by snakes, squirrels, and occasional house cats, most young wrens survive to flying age. Before dawn, parent wrens give a different note call and a succession of youngsters leave the nest. Often one clambers out and then, apparently terrified by the width of the world in view, turns and pushes back inside. Others respond to the vocal urging of the parents with no hesitation, jumping through the doorway and buzzing to the nearest bush on stubby wings that previously have had no room to beat. Ten baby wrens before 6:30 one morning, and three more the following day is our record number for one brood. The parents return once or twice later to the empty nest, as though to check that no youngster has been left behind.

Birds that nest in holes—in the habit followed by wrens, kingfishers, and swallows—have the greatest success in raising their young to the flying age. Only a third, on the average, are lost before the fledglings leave home. Small birds that feed their young in open nests, as robins and sparrows do, lose more than half to bad weather and predators before the young can fly. More vulnerable still are the quail and grouse, whose hatchlings follow them away from the nest as soon as the downy feathers dry; three out of four die before the survivors grow to be airborne. Apparently this high mortality is characteristic of the bird world. Dr. David Lack, the director of the Institute for Field Ornithology at Oxford University, estimates that only between 8 and 18 per cent of wild birds' eggs ordinarily give rise to adult birds. One would not have guessed at so low a rate of survival.

Mr. Raymond Middleton of Norristown, Pennsylvania, has brought us up to date on his experiences over the years in banding catbirds. By the time he had put numbered markers on 4760 of them, he had received information on about 6 per cent—those that had been caught again or found dead. Most had gone south for the winter and returned, many of them to the same few acres of land. Counting these homebodies, a total of 194 lived to be seen again one year after they were banded, 94 after two years, 30 after three, 14 after four, 7 after five, 3 after six, and 1 after seven. After the initial crash in numbers, seemingly due to inexperience among the fledglings, a half or more vanished annually without a trace, until all were gone. Yet, if catbirds wait until they are two years old to mate and raise a family, the future of their kind depends on a mature minority. The *average* lifespan for a catbird must be less than one and a half years.

The hazards of the first year of life are tremendous for any bird. It is the critical time of testing its inherited reactions against environmental odds. Only the survivors have a chance to benefit from experience. For most of our North American birds, those reactions include a complex response to season and geography that no scientist has yet been able to explain fully. As the time for migration nears, the bird may unconsciously measure the lengthening nights and shortening days, responding to autumn by eating heartily and storing fat as fuel for the coming trip. To take a bearing on true south, a bird's brain might be able to extrapolate the arc traced by the sun each day to find south at its highest point. An estimate of the height of the noonday sun above the horizon would give a measure of the latitude. With this information and some kind of an internal biological clock, a bird might navigate in a way comprehensible to man.

Eventually a scientist will discover how a bird knows when and which way to go. For now, we know only that this mysterious ability seems to be as much of the flier's heritage as its feathers. One year Professor William Rowan at the University of Alberta managed to gather 54 nestling crows and to raise them to the flying age in a cage building with no windows and no possible way for the nestlings to communicate with mature crows outdoors. He banded the youngsters, but kept them shut up a whole month after the last resident adult crow had been seen flying south. On November 8 he released the 54 captives. Edmonton and its environs offered no landmark they had seen, for the plains were snow-covered and the temperature sagged to zero Fahrenheit. Off they flew. But by November 20, cooperating birders had recaptured more than half of these banded crows. One had traveled 250 miles from the release point. All were well along in a narrow corridor between Edmonton and central Oklahoma, which is the wintering ground for almost every Alberta crow. Despite their inexperience and lack of leaders, they were on their way to join the flock in exactly the right direction.

So many millions of birds have now been given distinctive, numbered metal anklets that an enormous file of information about them is being kept up to date by the United States Fish and Wildlife Service at its research center in Laurel, Maryland. Tabulations from these data show how regularly various species head for their home range to breed and where they go to find food and shelter during northern winter, as well as a great deal about the yearly routes the myriad fliers take.

Often the breeding range and the winter range overlap, fooling people into believing that the same individual birds stay around all year. Generally these "permanent residents" prove to belong to a truly shifting population. Chickadees that nest near us and patronize our feeders in summer go south in autumn, just as more northerly chickadees come south to spend the winter here. For a while, twice a year, the changing of the guard brings new chickadees daily—as their leg bands show. Then the winter residents settle down, singing the same songs the summer chickadees did and taking their places at the food trays.

Long before the Fish and Wildlife Service had electronic computers to help with the data on banded birds, a biologist on the staff began plotting a separate map for each kind of bird. Each card in the file represented an individual bird which had been given an identifying band at one place and recovered at another. Some had been captured and released several times, each occasion adding another date and place to its dossier. Laboriously, Dr. Frederick C. Lincoln marked two or more dots for each bird to show where it had been. Then he joined these points with a line.

As the number of finished lines rose into the hundreds, Dr. Lincoln saw that they produced a pattern, as though the migrating birds flowed in great unmarked rivers between breeding and nesting areas. He called them "flyways" and described them in detail. Waterfowl, at least, seemed to restrict themselves individually to a single flyway for life. Accordingly, ducks and geese can be censused each year along the same routes, and hunting laws there adjusted so that a reasonable number will make the two-way trip unharmed.

Four great flyways carry the American migrants southward each autumn. For most, the spring return follows the same course. Route Number One is the "Atlantic flyway," used by waterfowl and land birds from New England, Greenland, and northern Canada as far west as the Mackenzie River. Converaging into a steady stream past Cape May, New Jersey, they follow the coast to Florida. Many fly onward to Cuba, Hispaniola, and Puerto Rico—the islands of the Greater Antilles. Ruby-throated hummingbirds cross from Florida to Yucatan and continue to their wintering areas in Mexico and Central America. Half a dozen other species, including the blue-winged teal, use the island chain of the West Indies like stepping stones, continuing around the eastern fringe of the Caribbean Sea to reach South America by way of Venezuela. Four times as many kinds fly straight from Cuba to Jamaica, then for 500 miles over open water to Colombia.

Route Number Two is the "Mississippi flyway," used by birds that nest in the broad drainage area of that great river, plus thousands more from Canada as far east as Baffin Land and as far west as the Yukon. Some Alaskan birds use this route too. For most of the waterfowl, the flyway ends in coastal marshes from western Florida to eastern Texas. Shore birds and land birds generally fly on, crossing to the peninsula of Yucatan and then fanning out into the tropical countries of Central America.

For 3000 miles of north-south travel, the Mississippi flyway offers well-watered fields and forests with no mountains to bar the way. At its southern end are offshore islands and river deltas which remain relatively undisturbed. Consequently, it is no surprise that more different kinds of birds and more individuals use this flyway than any of the other three.

Only slightly less popular is the "Central flyway," which serves the countless waterfowl of the Great Plains and northward to the Mackenzie Delta and eastern Alaska. The American widgeon, the pintail, and the redhead duck all use it regularly, traveling just east of the mountain barrier, between Texas or eastern Mexico and the home nesting areas in the northern plains and tundras. A surprising number of land birds from the Rocky Mountain region join these fliers from farther off, but few go farther than Vera Cruz along the Gulf of Mexico.

The "Pacific flyway" is far less popular. So close to the Pacific Ocean, its weather is much more uniform and few birds use it to travel far. Into it go fliers from the whole of Alaska, the Yukon, and western Canada, and states on the Pacific side of the Rockies. Along its length we meet black brant and rufous hummingbirds, violet-green swallows and Townsend's solitaire, the western tanager and the golden-crowned sparrow. Only a small number go beyond the forests of Guatemala.

When the great spring and fall migrations are in progress, an alert birder along any of these flyways has a wonderful opportunity to see birds that usually stay neither to nest nor to spend the winter. Particularly enthusiastic people make a point of spending a weekend or longer at Cape May, New Jersey, or visiting Hawk Mountain in Pennsylvania, or other famous centers where migrants pass in spectacular numbers. Those who have come some distance to witness the flyby generally realize that inherited guidance, geological topography, and weather patterns all combine to funnel birds into these distinctive corridors. Often, however, untraveled local citizens may firmly believe that a comparable armada would be encountered on the same date anywhere in the country. It *is* almost unbelievable that all of the hawks in a hundred square miles of territory can in a single day pass a point on the crest of some one mountain range, or circle by the skyful over the tip of one peninsula before setting out over open water toward land beyond. Often the migrants arriving at the barrier after midday wait until the following morning to start across. They resemble people waiting for a ferry—the far shore may actually be in sight, but the next day they will all go to it together.

The birder may often see the same migrants again by journeying south in winter or north in summer. Thousands of belted kingfishers and sparrow hawks perch on telephone wires along Florida highways at Christmas time, each bird waiting out the season of excessive cold in the North. From great areas of the United States and Canada they congregate together where they can find enough food to stay alive until spring permits them their homeward journey.

For the native birds of warm states and tropical countries, northern winter is a trying time. Hordes of migrant birds arrive and compete for the nourishment available. So long as they remain, the land may produce too few insects, fishes, fruits, and seeds to completely satisfy the hunger of so many mouths. There is no surplus to share with any young. Usually the native birds must wait until the visitors depart before beginning families of their own.

No comparable invasion of the Tropics occurs during the winter of the Southern Hemisphere, since neither the continents nor the islands on which birds nest get so cold as the comparable areas in the Northern Hemisphere. The number of birds is small, too, for there are no extensive southern tundras, and even the area of the south temperate latitudes is relatively limited. Indeed, the competition for food during the summer of the Southern Hemisphere is so slight that many plovers and sandpipers that nest in the Far North wing their way across the Tropics and spend *our* winter on the pampas of southern South America. The American golden plovers go there from the arctic tundras. Swainson's hawk, the cliff swallow, and the bobolink go almost as far.

In writing of his experiences with these North American migrants on the pampas a century ago, W. H. Hudson commented frequently that their colors were dull, their behavior predictable, and their numbers irregular from year to year. Probably he realized that each of these birds would moult and gain its colorful plumage before reaching its northern nesting grounds. There it would dance before its mate and follow the intricate inherited rituals that distinguish each kind. Migrants on the southbound trip, and during the wintering months, wear generally the somber colors of juveniles. It is when they are headed for home and preparations for raising a new family that the birder sees them at their best. They are all dressed up, with somewhere definite to go—each to its previous nesting area, or to the place where it hatched from an egg.

Robin
Turdus migratorius
Length 8½" to 10½"

CHAPTER TWO

FAMILIAR SPECIES

IN NORTH AMERICA, ALMOST EVERYONE KNOWS THAT A ROBIN'S EGG IS robin's-egg blue. But then, **robins** are probably the best known of all our birds. They build their bulky nests of grass and mud so close to houses that the egg shells, discarded a certain distance from the nest after the chicks hatch, become almost as familiar as the birds themselves.

From Alaska to Georgia, from California to Newfoundland and Labrador, these birds find building sites on front porches, on horizontal bends in the downspouts from eavestroughs, in the crotches of low trees, or in the middle of decorative shrubs. There they incubate their three to five blue eggs and feed their fast-growing young until the freckle-chested offspring can fly and follow the parents, begging loudly for more food. Often the youngster is as large as it will ever be before it begins finding its own earthworms, insects, berries, and other fruits.

By September, all the robins in a region become sociable and begin to travel south. Many of the most northern birds go just across the international line into the United States, replacing others that have gone to Florida or well down into Mexico for the winter. By early spring they are homebound again, reaching the northern states by mid-March, the southern extremes of Alaska and Labrador by the end of the month, and their farthest nesting territories in early May even before the ice and snow are gone. Once on home ground, the male robin finds a prominent lookout perch, puffs out his orange breast, straightens his gray back, spreads his tail slightly to show its white corners, and opens his yellow beak slightly while his white throat vibrates in tempo with his cheerful whistled song. This is his claim to territory. So well liked is the bird and his notes that Connecticut, Michigan, Virginia, and Wisconsin have all chosen the robin to represent their state.

Robins are actually a kind of thrush, as are their smaller, gentler kin, the bluebirds. Both robins and bluebirds migrate in flocks by day, whereas the other thrushes travel singly at night. Bluebirds have sweeter voices, a soft warbled whistle. They utter it on the wing and while sitting in the sun on a conspicuous perch, watching for insects they can fly down to and catch in the grass. Unlike other thrushes, bluebirds choose a hole to nest in and line it with fine fibers from various plants. Yet their eggs show the characteristic pale blue color of eggs from other thrushes, and their young wear spotted feathers on the breast.

We have often wondered whether Maeterlinck had an actual bird in mind when he wrote *The Bluebird*. There are none in the Old World, though North America is enriched with three different kinds. Bluest is the all-blue male of the **mountain bluebird,** which is sky-blue on crown and back, wings and tail and paler elsewhere; his mate is mostly grayish brown. We have found them nesting under the eaves of outbuildings in Jackson Hole, Wyoming, and elsewhere between the southwestern deserts and Alaska, mostly at elevations between 5000 and 12,000 feet.

Most familiar of the bluebirds is the **eastern bluebird,** not found west of the Rocky Mountains. It ranges into Canada about as far north as major cities have been built, and eastward to Bermuda, south to Florida and the coast of Texas. As adults, both sexes have a bright rust-red throat and chest, white underparts, and intensely blue wings. The male sports a solid blue crown and back, while those of his mate are a less conspicuous gray. After consuming countless insects from early spring until autumn, they and their

Mountain Bluebird
Sialia currucoides
Length 6½″ to 7″

Eastern Bluebird
Sialia sialis
Length 6½″ to 7½″

North American Birds

young show a hunger for berries and other fruits as they travel toward the Gulf of Mexico and into Mexico itself for the winter. Those that go farthest have a chance to meet both the mountain bluebirds and also the **western bluebirds** of lowlands between the Canadian border, the Pacific coast, and the major mountains. Both sexes of western bluebirds have a rusty chest and a reddish brown over the wings along the back. The male's head and throat are all dark blue; his mate is brownish gray. For some reason, the western and mountain bluebirds sing mostly at daybreak, but their song is typical of the species, without a harsh note anywhere.

The "caw" of the **American crow** ranks among the best known of bird calls, but its inflections are so numerous and significant that they seem to approach a spoken language. These powerful, social birds serve as valuable scavengers over all but the most northern parts of the continent and the southwestern deserts. (Over the deserts, too, they often travel on migration into Mexico.) Seldom gliding, except to descend where their sharp eyes have sighted food, crows flap across the sky like animated silhouettes. Even their nests, usually in the form of a platform of sticks high in a dead tree, are easily seen from below. There the wary parents can watch for danger in all directions, just as the lookout in the "crow's-nest" on a ship can scan the horizon.

Western Bluebird
Sialia mexicana
Length 6½" to 7"

Common Crow
Corvus brachyrhynchos
Length 17″ to 21″

Raven
Corvus corax
Length 21½″ to 27″

In the Far North and the American West, a still larger all-black bird has become common and may be extending its range. It is the **raven,** which spreads its broad wings as much as 56 inches tip to tip and often soars above pastures and ranch lands, looking for carrion, injured animals, rodents, and grasshoppers to pounce on. Its gigantic appetite gives us the adjective "ravenous," for the same bird is well known in the Old World too from the coasts of Iceland south to North Africa and eastward into Siberia. Our ravens presumably are identical with those that now fly around Mount Ararat (16,900 feet high) in eastern Turkey, where Genesis records Noah as having "sent forth a raven, which went to and fro, until the waters were dried up from off the earth."

We share quite naturally with the great expanse of Eurasia a smaller relative of the crow—the **black-billed magpie.** As this common bird in our western states flies over open country from its feeding places on the ground, its long green tail streams out behind and the clean white areas on each side of its back (like its underparts) contrast sharply with its all-black head and throat. Green on its wings near the body merely serves to accentuate the black-edged white feathers beyond as they sweep up and down, propelling the bird along. Somewhere in the history of British folklore are the events that led Englishmen to apply the nickname Mag (for Margaret) to the bird they called the pie, and to refer to any animal or human costume with a contrasty pattern as "pied."

Black-Billed Magpie
Pica pica
Length 17½" to 22"

North American Birds

Magpies and jays, although closely related to ravens and crows, have comparatively short wings, reaching only to the base of the tail rather than approaching its tip. Seemingly in consequence, their flight is more flashing, and they dart among the branches of trees at high speed. Certainly they take advantage of this skill to escape when people become irritated by their raucous chatter or when they choose to rob the nests of other birds. But when the total diet is analyzed, all these related birds are seen to do more good than bad. The familiar **blue jay** so common east of the Rocky Mountains often saves the lives of other animals by screaming at the top of its voice at the sight of any predator in the half-mile territory around its nesting site. They add more color and excitement than most of our native birds.

Blue Jay
Cyanocitta cristata
Length 11″ to 12″

Often we are amazed at the persistence birds show in watching any wandering house cat that might molest their nests or young. Even if no blue jays are around to help, robins and catbirds take up posts as sentinels and produce cries that are easy to interpret. The robin's *churk* and the catbird's *mew* have the same significance. At safer times the **catbirds** slip silently among the shrubbery, finding insects upon the foliage and the ground. Or a catbird will perch within sight of its nest, whistling sounds of its own invention and mimicking the calls of other birds. Its pattern of song changes continuously, but draws attention to the slim gray body with its black cap and rusty red patch under the dark tail.

Catbird
Dumetella carolinensis
Length 8½″ to 9¼″

North American Birds

If the imitative calls are loud and each is repeated twice, the singer almost invariably turns out to be the larger **brown thrasher.** It is a cinnamon-colored bird with rows of black streaks on its white breast. Thrashers are common east of the Rockies and central Texas, nesting as far north as southern Canada and wintering to the coast of the Gulf of Mexico. Catbirds range more widely—to southern British Columbia and the maritime provinces of Canada, and to Bermuda. In winter some of them travel far down into the West Indies and to Colombia.

A songster that is still more accomplished and, like the nightingale of Europe, often displays its abilities on moonlit nights is the American **mockingbird.** Even by moonlight, the flash of white on its wings and the sides of its tail lets us recognize a gray mockingbird in flight. Its clear voice is equally distinctive for, while it changes its tune frequently, it commonly repeats each phrase several times. On occasion, its imitation of other bird calls is so nearly perfect that an attentive listener cannot be sure whether the song he has heard is

Brown Thrasher
Toxostoma rufum
Length 10½" to 12"

Familiar Species

the real thing or a mockingbird's facsimile. This uncertainty adds to the challenge of identifying birds by ear all over the territory defended by mockingbirds—an area stretching from California to southern New England and south to Yucatan and the Virgin Islands.

Mockingbird
Mimus polyglottos
Length 9″ x 11″

North American Birds

The variety of bird calls is almost endless, and yet distinctive patterns are audible. A lisping, high-pitched note—perhaps a little higher than the highest on a piano keyboard—from several birds in the same tree generally comes from waxwings, crested fruit-eaters whose every feather is always in sleek position. **Bohemian waxwings** are wanderers common to northern parts of the Old World and in America from Alaska and western Canada southward in winter into

Bohemian Waxwing
Bombycilla garrula
Length 7½″ to 8¾″

Familiar Species

the western United States. Occasionally they stray eastward to northern New England, where otherwise the waxwings are all strictly New World denizens—the **cedar waxwings**—with almost identical calls. The waxy material for which these birds are named is a strange adornment of the tips of their shorter wing feathers. It closely resembles the cherry-red wax formerly used for sealing letters and other documents.

Cedar Waxwing
Bombycilla cedrorum
Length 6½″ to 8″

North American Birds

For its size, none of our birds can produce as much volume of song as the little **house wren,** four and a quarter inches long from point of beak to tip of upturned stubby tail. Quick and aggressive, these wrens drive other birds from the area around their chosen nesting sites, and repeat their buzzing one-second songs about twelve times each minute from before daybreak until hunger or parental duties take them elsewhere. Some of our friends claim it is easier to sleep near a foghorn than near a house wren which is claiming a piece of property outside the bedroom window. People in Ohio must react differently, for they have chosen the house wren as their state bird. In the American Southeast, particularly in winter, its territory over-laps with that of the slightly larger Carolina wren—state bird of South Carolina—which southerners claim says *teakettle* loud and quickly, four to six times at half-second intervals, repeating the call eight to thirteen times a minute.

Far more in keeping with the size of the bird are the calls of the various blackbirds, orioles, and near relatives. Of approximately the dimensions of a robin, some larger, some smaller, they differ in songs and color patterns so much that it is easy to tell them apart. Loud

House Wren
Troglodytes aedon
Length 4½" to 5¼"

Familiar Species

throaty whistles from the top of a tall tree, such as a New England elm, tell us that the **Baltimore orioles** are back to weave their amazing pendant sock-like nests. They find suitable supports in shade trees east of the Rocky Mountains and from the populated parts of Canada south to the mouth of the Mississippi. In winter they find a satisfying mixture of insects and fruits in southeastern Mexico and warm countries all the way to Colombia. Their link to Maryland, of which they are the state bird, came about because their contrasting black and orange color matched the family coat of arms belonging to George Calvert, the first Baron Baltimore, who founded Maryland.

Baltimore Oriole
Icterus galbula
Length 7″ to 9″

North American Birds

In the western part of their range, they overlap and hybridize with **Bullock's orioles,** birds of the West and much of Mexico. In the East, the Baltimores manage to minimize competition with a rather similar bird, the orchard oriole, which frequents smaller trees and the edges of woodlands, producing a more melodious and continuous flute-like whistling. But it is much harder to see because its body is brick red where the Baltimore's is brilliant orange. The tail is dark, not flashily edged with orange-yellow. In all of these orioles, the male is the conspicuous sex. The females and juveniles lack the black markings and trend toward olive drab or yellowish green or pale grayish with an orange tint.

Bullock's Oriole
Icterus bullockii
Length 7″ to 8½″

Bobolinks too, show this marked sexual difference during the breeding season. The males that bubble with song, loudly defending the vacant lot or grassy field around the grass tuft their mates have chosen as a place to conceal a nest, are blackbirds only in terms of their dark "basecoat." The back of the head is bright solid golden yellow, the shoulders and back white. All these markings show plainly while the male flutters and sings, distracting attention from his plain brownish-yellow female. Yet when the young are raised, he moults to winter plumage resembling hers. The whole family flies off to central South America as far as northern Argentina.

Bobolink
Dolichonyx oryzivorous
Length 6½″ to 8″

North American Birds

The meadowlarks, close kin to the Bobolinks, stay much closer to home during the cold months. The **eastern meadowlark** is back by the first of April in the northern limits of its range, in Canada from Manitoba to Nova Scotia. Its clear whistled song, and its butter-yellow breast marked with a black V, differ only in details from those of the western meadowlark. Just west of the Mississippi the two kinds overlap in their nesting distribution. In winter, many of both go to Mexico, but only the eastern meadowlarks spread still farther southward—into Central America and the West Indies. Small yet important differences in food habits—the eastern meadowlark eats more insects and the western one more weed seeds and grain—prevent these similar and related birds from seriously competing with one another.

Eastern Meadowlark
Sturnella magna
Length 9″ to 11″

Familiar Species

The **California quail** is widely familiar west of the Sierra Nevada since it so often visits suburban lawns in the early morning and late evening—after the sprinking system has brought out the slugs and insects and made plant buds especially firm. Generally, from the covey of 20 to 30 individuals an experienced male will scout ahead, perhaps fly up into a low tree for a better view, and then signal all clear. The others run out from cover into the open and begin foraging while he keeps watch. Before long another adult male will explore in a new direction and, at his call, the old lookout can rejoin the group to feed. The males have a chestnut cap bordered by black-and-white lines on brow and sides of the head, a black throat with a white border, and a smoke-blue breast that meets brown underparts flecked with white. The females and young lack the clear markings on head and throat but have the same little jaunty topknot which bobs forward above the beak.

California Quail
Lophortyx californicus
Length 9½″ to 11″

North American Birds

The most widely familiar quail of all is the **bobwhite.** Throughout its range in the southeastern quarter of the continent, its loud whistled call invites imitation: *Bob—Bob-WHITE*. A bird of the woodland borders, its numbers increased spectacularly as the colonists began clearing the forest. It thrives among underbrush, eating a great variety of insect pests in summer and weed seeds in winter. When the daylight grows dim, all members of a covey huddle together in a compact circle, facing out, with tails together. They share their warmth without getting in one another's way for, at the slightest disturbance, the whole covey explodes into the air—every bird flying in a different direction. This was a surprising discovery to the pioneer naturalist, Mark Catesby, who called them "American partridge" (the bobwhite is still called "partridge" in the southeastern United States). *That Quail, Robert* was a female bobwhite, known by a name for the bird that is used widely in New England.

Bobwhite
Colinus virginianus
Length 8½″ to 10½″

No such admiration is lavished on the glossy iridescent **common grackles,** which are generally abundant in farmland and suburban communities east of the Rocky Mountains and western Texas. "Grackle" is an imitation of their harsh voices, which encompass many guttural cries as well as a medley of squeaky whistles that have been compared to the sounds of a rusty hinge on an old door. West of Lake Michigan, the common blackbird of similar localities is the slightly smaller Brewer's blackbird. In both kinds, the eyes of adults are a conspicuous white; those of the young are brown until October.

Common Grackle
Quiscalus quiscula
Length 11″ to 13″

North American Birds

Least admirable of the blackbirds, because of its parasitic habits, is the **brown-headed cowbird.** It is often found in abundance from coast to coast, and from northern Mexico well north into Canada. As long ago as 1809, Alexander Wilson wrote to his friend William Bartram that he had "every reason to believe that this bird never builds itself a nest, but, like the cuckoo of Europe, drops its eggs into the nests of other birds." The female is mouse-gray, and resembles a sparrow—except when she is busy removing eggs from an unguarded nest and putting her own in their place. Both sexes of cowbirds flock together, walking in search of seeds, the blue-black, brown-headed males often pausing to spread wings and tail while uttering an unmusical squeak.

We might give cowbirds more credit for the good they do in eating harmful insects and weed seeds, if they at least chose nests of

Brown-Headed Cowbird
Molothrus ater
Length 7" to 8"

birds their own size. But they usually pick smaller birds, particularly warblers and sparrows. Far too often the foster parents are harassed by a hungry young cowbird whose overgrown existence costs the lives of several of its nest-mates. One kind of warbler parasitized—the **yellow warbler** or "wild canary"—seems to recognize a cowbird's egg as too white, too big, too brown-speckled. This warbler, which tolerates people and often builds its cup-shaped nest of silver-gray plant fibers in a shrub near a house, simply installs a new floor. Adding a little to the rim, it lays a new clutch of greenish-white eggs flecked with brownish-purple. As many as five new floors and new sets of eggs may go in if cowbirds are persistent. By then the summer is far along, and the yellow warbler parents have trouble getting their own offspring ready for migration in time for the autumn flight to the West Indies and tropical America.

Yellow Warbler
Dendroica petechia
Length 5"

North American Birds

The sparrows and juncos, finches and buntings that are so often victimized by cowbirds near human habitations are all members of the largest family of North American birds, the family Fringillidae. All resemble cowbirds in having a short, conical, powerful beak useful in cracking hard seeds. They nest in clumps of weeds, among shrubs, in trees, or just on the ground under low arching grass.

Best known of these little birds that measure between 4¼ and 6 inches from tip of tail to end of beak is the **American goldfinch.** From coast to coast and from southern Canada in summer to northeastern Mexico and Florida in winter, it flits across fields as though following the ups and downs of a roller coaster. At the top of each rise it calls *poTAto-chip!* in a high sweet voice. Or it perches on a weed stem and shrills *zweee*. During the nesting season the adult male has a jet black cap, black wings and tail but otherwise is golden yellow; at other seasons his colors seem faded like those of his mate.

American Goldfinch
Spinus tristis
Length 5″ to 5½″

When the goldfinches move south for the winter, the **common red-polls** often replace them at suburban bird feeders all across the United States toward the Gulf of Mexico. The red forehead and brown-streaked rump are easy to recognize, and the male has a beautiful rosy breast as well. Redpolls have the same undulating flight and sociable ways as goldfinches, and were among the winter birds the American colonists recognized, since redpolls are also native to the British Isles, Iceland, northern Scandinavia, and Switzerland. Their songs, however, seem harsh by comparison with the

Common Redpoll
Acanthis flammea
Length 5" to 5½"

North American Birds

melodious warbling of the somewhat similar **house finch** of the western United States and Mexico and the more widely distributed **purple finch.** In both, the male is red to wine-colored on head, chest, and rump, whereas his mate and young birds resemble large brown sparrows with many coarse brown markings on a white breast and throat. The purple finch nests across Canada and southward in coastal states to California and Virginia.

House Finch
Carpodacus mexicanus
Length 5″ to 5¾″

Purple Finch
Carpodacus purpureus
Length 5½″ to 6¼″

Getting to know the real sparrows is an art in itself. But those that come close to human communities, to suburban feeders, and to cultivated fields or road margins provide the easy beginning. We get to be critical of little things, such as whether its breast is plain, or has a single spot in the middle, or a whole series of streaked spots. The plain ones we see most often are the friendly little **chipping sparrow** and the field sparrow. The chippers' song is a prolonged series of rapid musical chips without inflection. It has a black beak, a rusty cap, a conspicuous white line over the eye, but throat, sides, and underparts are ash-gray. Chipping sparrows return every spring from wintering areas in the southern states and throughout Mexico and begin hopping around on the ground, hunting for insects and nesting sites among the bushes, anywhere from southern Alaska to Newfoundland, down to Georgia, east Texas, and Baja California.

Chipping Sparrow
Spizella passerina
Length 5" to 5½"

North American Birds

Field sparrows are missing from most of Canada and from west of the Rocky Mountains, but tell of their presence in their central and eastern range by a slightly slurred chipping sound that begins slowly and speeds up. The singer has a pink beak, a brown cap, a narrow white ring around the eye, and a pastel brown wash over the rest of the head, throat, and underparts.

Field Sparrow
Spizella pusilla
Length 5¼" to 6"

The one-spot sparrows of widest distribution are the **tree sparrows,** which nest far north in Alaska and Canada but spend the winter among people in all of the United States except the Far West and the South. They sing on their nesting grounds where few are around to hear them, and briefly again on spring migration while feeding among suburban trees and hedges. When a tree sparrow is pecking away at seeds on the bird feeder outside a window, you can admire its feathered coat and notice that the upper half of its

Tree Sparrow
Spizella arborea
Length 6″ to 6½″

North American Birds

beak is dark gray, the underpart a pale pink. The only other one-spot sparrow, the **lark sparrow,** has a yellow beak. The male's head is attractively marked with chestnut-red ear patches, reminding us of the markings on a quail. The lark sparrow is primarily a bird of the central states, spreading in summer northward into the Canadian prairie provinces and in winter into Central America; to the eastern coast of America it is a rare visitor, perhaps blown off course by storms.

Both the tree sparrow and the lark sparrow have a white edge to the tail. So does the vesper sparrow, which differs conspicuously in this way from the other two small brownish sparrows with dark-spotted breasts that come commonly where people live. Often the vesper sparrows flit ahead of you as you walk along a country road. But in the eastern United States they are less common now that farming areas have shrunk in size. Still, they can be heard in early morning and evening, singing a complex musical song that starts low and slow, then rises in pitch and speed.

Song sparrows and savannah sparrows sometimes test the birder's skill, for both are brown birds with dark-spotted breasts and brown tails. And an immature song sparrow lacks the adults' distinctive big dark splotch in the middle of the breast. But, at any age, a song sparrow has a longer tail, rounded at the end, which it pumps up and down while flying. It perches often as high above the ground as the second story of a building. It is from such a lookout that the adults sing their bright little messages, starting in a high key and descending. Henry Thoreau imitated their phrasing with *Maids! Maids! Maids! Hang up your teakettle-ettle-ettle.* Over the years the interpretation has turned into *Hip! Hip! Hip! Hurray boys, spring is here.* We can hear it near nest sites in northern states and in Canada from Newfoundland across to Alaska. For winter, song sparrows travel as far as northern Mexico. **Savannah sparrows,** by contrast, have shorter tails notched at the tip. They are birds of the grasslands that ordinarily sing their buzzy songs from no higher than a fence top. They nest all across the Arctic in the New World and as far south as Guatemala, wintering along east and west coasts, in the Gulf States and the northern West Indies.

A junco is actually a plain little sparrow with a dark gray head, frequently with unmarked gray on much of the wings and body,

Lark Sparrow
Chondestes grammacus
Length 5½″ to 6½″

Song Sparrow
Melospiza melodia
Length 5″ to 6¾″

Savannah Sparrow
Passerculus sandwichensis
Length 5¼″ to 6″

Slate-Colored Junco
Junco hyemalis
Length 6″ to 6½″

but with white edges to the tail. The common **slate-colored junco** is the small gray snow bird that spends the winter across most of the United States and southern Canada, then departs to nest far north from Alaska to Labrador where few birders hear its musical trilled song. From the Great Plains west to the Pacific coast, the **Oregon junco** turns up in the suburbs and on farmlands when winter becomes too severe in its nesting territory at higher elevations and northward up the Pacific coastal slopes. This western junco has a reddish-brown back but, where the color extends over its wings and onto its sides, it may be pink in a broad stripe contrasting with the white undersides. It was such a pink-sided junco that we watched in the Jackson Hole country of Wyoming, tending its nestlings on the ground in an open bit of pine woods, while we sat about three feet away and counted fat green caterpillars going into the wide-open mouths.

Oregon Junco
Junco oreganus
Length 5″ to 6″

North American Birds

Some of our more familiar birds we notice because of their loud calls, others because they sit on telephone wires and let us make their acquaintance if only in silhouette against the sky. One of these birds that comes scratching on the ground under our shrubbery and calling in a loud clear whistle is the **rufous-sided towhee,** which some of our friends call a "ground robin." Where the male is black, on head and throat, wings, back, and tail, his mate is brown. Both have reddish-brown along the sides, with white below, on the wings and the tail. Familiar birds in the more settled parts of Canada, they nest far south, except in the central states. Indians knew them as *chewink,* which is a good imitation of the call with which pairs keep in touch despite intervening foliage. The full song is *DRINK-your-TEEEEE,* often abbreviated to the last two syllables—*tow-HEEEE.* In the Southwest, the less colorful **brown towhee** scratches for food in the same way, but repeats monotonously, *SIP-SIP-SIP-SIP-INK-INK-INK-INK-INK.*

Rufous-Sided Towhee
Pipilo erythrophthalmus
Length 7½" to 8¾"

Brown Towhee
Pipilo fuscus
Length 8¼″ to 10″

North American Birds

Most spectacular of these loud-voiced American birds are the grosbeaks which are only slightly smaller than robins and show such great differences in coloration among males, females, and juveniles that a beginning birder might easily conclude there were three different kinds for each species. The favorite grosbeak is certainly the **cardinal,** which is the only one with an impressive crest that can be raised and lowered. The male is bright red (even including his beak), except for black around the beak and for his black eyes. The female has a red beak and black eyes, too, but her feathers are olive-green. Her wings and tail are reddish and her back gray. Juvenile cardinals wear an almost uniform reddish-gray; even their beaks are dusky. Over southernmost Ontario and most of the eastern United States and Mexico, these handsome birds brighten the day with their clear whistled *CHEER, CHEER, What-CHEER, What-CHEER, What-CHEER!*

Equally attracted to the feeding shelf by sunflower seeds are the **evening grosbeaks,** which come irregularly in flocks and then quarrel over food. Females and juveniles are like the males in having a huge pale beak, with which they can shell seeds at an astonishing pace, and in having black on wings and forked tail. The male is strikingly yellow otherwise, except for a large patch of white on his wings, and a gray to black wash over his nape, his lower head and shoulders, and from his chin part way down his breast. Our eyes automatically follow these gaudy noisy birds, paying less attention to those that are merely gray washed with olive-yellow where the males are so bright. Until recently, evening grosbeaks were regarded as

Cardinal
Richmondena cardinalis
Length 8″ to 9″

western birds, and they still nest mostly west and north of the Mississippi valley. But now many are breeding across Canada and up the St. Lawrence, wintering south to Georgia. At the same time the cardinals have been moving north, until southern Ontario has been included in their normal range.

Evening Grosbeak
Hesperiphona vespertina
Length 7½″ to 8½″

North American Birds

The rosy bib of the **rose-breasted grosbeak** is a mark of the male only; his wings are also rosy underneath. He perches and calls loudly like a robin with a special, close-clipped accent. All but his bib is black or white—the white on beak, wing bars, and underside, and below the tail. His mate appears to be an overgrown sparrow with a strangely heavy beak, white wing bars, and dark brown streaks upon the breast. Her wings are lined with orange-yellow, which is displayed whenever she flies. While she builds her nest in a shrub or tree anywhere between five and 20 feet above the ground, the male usually perches far higher and sings as though about to exhaust himself. These birds provide a climax to the spring migration when they have come all the way from the West Indies and Central America.

Rose-Breasted Grosbeak
Pheucticus ludovicianus
Length 7″ to 8½″

Familiar Species

In the southeastern states, a glimpse of a bird that is mostly deep bright blue is not enough to know for sure whether it is a male **blue grosbeak** or a male **indigo bunting.** The grosbeak is twice as heavy, with a bigger beak and two rust-colored wing bars. His voice is a warble and he usually hides in a thicket while singing. His mate has orange wing bars and the same big beak, which distinguish her from any sparrow. Blue grosbeaks nest from coast to coast, as far north as South Dakota, whereas almost all indigo buntings are at home east of the Mississippi, northward into southern Canada. Both of these kinds of neighborly birds change to dull feathers as they travel toward the American tropics for the winter.

Indigo Bunting
Passerina cyanea
Length 5¼″ to 5¾″

Blue Grosbeak
Guiraca caerulea
Length 6″ to 7½″

North American Birds

Generally we see an indigo bunting perched on a wire as he sings in double whistles, waiting for his mate to arrive from the South or guarding while she tends her nest in the shrubbery. This same exposed perch appeals also to the **lazuli buntings** of the western states and the painted buntings we meet wintering in Florida, although their nesting grounds are mostly westward around the Gulf of Mexico and down into Latin America. The male lazuli is paler blue than the indigo and has enough buffy wash on his breast and sides to suggest a bluebird; his white wing bars distinguish him as well as his sparrow size. His mate has the wing bars and blue on the back and tail, yet still resembles a sparrow. A painted bunting is like nothing else native to our continent. Even the female is a brilliant yellow-green. Her mate combines a bright blue head, red eye ring, red underparts and rump, yellowish-green back, and a combination of all these colors on his wings. Yet, just as in the Tropics, this multiplicity of colors makes the painted bunting hard to see; our eyes focus on one hue, one area, at a time and fail to put them all together into the shape of a bird.

Lazuli Bunting
Passerina amoena
Length 5″ to 5½″

Familiar Species

Surely man is not alone in looking out for birds that perch on overhead wires along the roads. One species that uses this vantage point must be a terror for everything the size of a mouse or a sparrow. The **loggerhead shrike** of southern Canada and all of the United States might be mistaken for a plump mockingbird. The northern shrike, which ranges from the Far North into the northern states, is

Loggerhead Shrike
Lanius ludovicianus
Length 9″

even more similar. On closer view, each is seen to have a black mask-like marking through the eyes and a hooked tip to the stout beak that marks it as a predator. A shrike may hover over a grasshopper before pouncing. Seeking a mouse or a small bird, it usually comes in undulating flight with wingbeats too fast to count. Old-timers knew shrikes as "butcher birds" because, when prey is plentiful (such as during migration time), shrikes kill more than they can eat immediately and impale the surplus on the sharp thorns of hawthorn or locust trees or on the nearest barbed-wire fence. When a shrike perches on a wire, other birds of smaller size usually disappear. Probably this predator mainly catches small birds and mammals that are unwary due to illness, accident, or old age.

Without a shrike around, wires are favorite perches for various kinds of swallows. They socialize by the dozen, chittering and preening themselves, each individual darting off at intervals to capture a few small flying insects before returning to the group. All are slim little birds with tiny feet, long pointed wings, and a wide mouth tipped by a short flat beak. Their speed and aerial acrobatics have delighted people for thousands of years.

Barn Swallow
Hirundo rustica
Length 6″ to 7½″

Familiar Species

The only kind of swallow with a long "swallowtail" is the **barn swallow,** which long ago began benefitting from human company by building its mud nests inside barns—usually atop a beam or rafter close to an open door or window. The male has a chestnut throat and forehead, while his mate and young are paler. The **cliff swallows** plaster their mud nests on the outside, sometimes around the same building, high under the eaves. Each nest is gourd-shaped, with a doorway in the side. Cliff swallows of both sexes have a rusty patch on the rump, and square tails. **Tree swallows** hunt for natural cavities to nest in, and will often compete with house wrens and bluebirds for a man-made bird house. West of the Rocky Mountains we

Cliff Swallow
Petrochelidon pyrrhonota
Length 5″ to 6″

Tree Swallow
Iridoprocne bicolor
Length 5″ to 6″

North American Birds

have to look carefully at these quick fliers, for a tree swallow's white breast is worn by the **violet-green swallows** as well, and the notching of the tail is very similar. A violet-green has white above the eyes, and the white of its underside goes around its body in front of the black tail until only a narrow dark stripe is left down the back. This bird winters in Mexico but goes as far north as Alaska for the nesting season. The tree swallow, which has no white above the eyes and is green all the way down the back to the tail, is like the barn swallow and the cliff swallow in breeding from coast to coast and still farther north. It winters in the Gulf States or Latin America.

Violet-Green Swallow
Tachycineta thalassina
Length 5″ to 5½″

Familiar Species

The biggest swallow in North America is the **purple martin,** a colonial nesting bird that spends the winter in South America. Now that there are so few old trees with suitable tree holes, martins have become almost dependent on people who put up artificial apartment houses specifically for them, with rooms six by six inches and an outside door to each about an inch and a half in diameter. They pay their rent by ravaging the local insect population. The male martins are so dark purple they appear black from a distance. Their mates and young are dark brownish on back, with some gray below. Together they make so much racket, sometimes even at night, that it is well to place the martin house well away from your own, in the midst of an open space. Too many nearby trees tend to cramp the martins' socializing in the air.

Purple Martin
Progne subis
Length 7½″ to 8½″

North American Birds

Most pugnacious of the neighborly birds that perch on wires are the kingbirds, which birders group with the meek little phoebes as "tyrant flycatchers." Flycatchers they certainly are, flying horizontally and then plummeting to snap up a good-sized insect. The **eastern kingbird** has the broader range, extending to Puget Sound and the fringe of Canada's Northwest Territories as well as to the Maritime Provinces and Florida. In winter it goes to western South America, still marked by the broad white tip to its square-ended tail. It is always ready to make a wide detour to attack a vulture or a crow, even to grasping the larger bird by the back feathers between its flapping wings and pecking at its neck and head! The **western kingbird** has white feathers at the sides of its tail and comes as far east as Lake Erie. It winters in southern Mexico and Central America. Perhaps because trees are scarce in many areas it occupies, it

Eastern Kingbird
Tyrannus tyrannus
Length 8½″ to 9″

Western Kingbird
Tyrannus verticalis
Length 8″ to 9½″

nests quite often under the eaves of ranch buildings. The eastern kingbird, by contrast, usually chooses a tall tree stump or a shrub as the site for its bulky nest, which is rough on the outside but a trim cup inside.

Most summers we hear a phoebe before we see the bird. Although its voice is gentle, it has an impatient sound—like that of a spouse waiting for a tardy mate. *FEE-bee!* Then, with a rising inflection: *Fee-BEE?*, over and over, and never followed by *Dammit, where are you?* All the while, the phoebe will be perching on a low branch somewhere, watching for a flying insect to dart after. Unlike other flycatchers, phoebes all wag their tails down and up at a leisurely pace, as a distinctive signal rather than a means for regaining lost balance. When possible, the **eastern phoebe** nests under bridges near small streams, anywhere east of the Rockies from northwestern Alberta to the Maritime Provinces of Canada and south to the Texas coast. In winter we see these birds in the Gulf States and eastern Mexico.

Eastern Phoebe
Sayornis phoebe
Length 6½" to 7"

Say's Phoebe
Sayornis saya
Length 7″ to 8″

Black Phoebe
Sayornis nigricans
Length 6¼″ to 7″

Familiar Species

Only in its winter range does it overlap with **Say's phoebe,** a rust-colored bird instead of a mostly gray one. Ranchers from Alaska to Mexico and the Pacific coast imitate its calls as *chu-WEER* and, less often, *pippety-CHEE.* In the far Southwest, the **black phoebe** perches in shady places, calling its name in a high thin voice and wagging its white-edged tail. Its breast and head, back and wings, and the central portion of its tail are all dull black. Otherwise it is white below, and resembles a giant junco.

One other bird makes a whistled call that can be written *fee-bee,* rising in pitch on the first note and down again on the second, stressing both about equally. It is a spring sound of the **black-capped chickadee,** which nests and winters across the continent from Alaska to Newfoundland. With its black cap, bib, and eyes and white cheeks and side of the head, this rusty gray midget will often take food from an outstretched hand. Almost everyone gets to recognize its happy-sounding *CHICK-a-dee-dee.* But imitating this call well enough to summon the bird is not as easy as whistling *fee-bee* at the right time of year.

Black-Capped Chickadee
Parus atricapillus
Length 4¾″ to 5½″

Ruby-Throated Hummingbird
Archilochus colubris
Length 3″ to 3¾″

Rufous Hummingbird
Selasphorus rufus
Length 3⅓″ to 3.9″

Our only birds smaller than chickadees are the hummingbirds, whose buzzing wings can carry them backward, upward, and even sidewise as well as forward and down. By preference the hummer comes from underneath a pendant flower and extends its slender beak into its depths to sip nectar, taking any small insects at the same time. East of the Mississippi only the **ruby-throated hummers** come, and only the males wear the brilliant ruby-red iridescent colors. The female does all the nest-building, choosing a horizontal branch on which to build her snug little lichen-covered cup. Alone she watches her two pea-sized eggs, feeds the chicks, and gets them to fly. West of the Rockies, from Alaska southward, the slightly larger **rufous hummingbird** corresponds in many ways to the ruby-throated. The male rufous has an orange throat and chest, colors that are replaced by gray and green on his mate. Both wear orange on the rump and tail. In California, **Anna's hummers** join the rufous at flowers around human habitations. The male Anna's has a rose-red crown and throat. Generally the female's black-flecked gray throat has a red patch at the center.

Anna's Hummingbird
Calypte anna
Length 3½″ to 4″

Mourning Dove
Zenaidura macroura
Length 11″ to 13″

Ground Dove
Columbigallina passerina
Length 6″ to 6¾″

Just as the whirr of a hummingbird's wings tells us that the bird is near, so can the whistle of longer and more pointed wings call attention to a flock of doves. Most widespread of native North American kinds is the **mourning dove,** which comes to farms and suburbs for grain and weed seeds as far north as Alaska and Nova Scotia, and south into Central America. Its long pointed tail with a thin line of white on the sides distinguishes the mourning dove even in flight from the tiny doves of the South and Southwest. There the smallest is the common **ground dove,** which has a short dark rounded tail. Slightly larger is the Inca dove, with a longer rounded tail that is white around the end. Both of these little doves flash dull reddish areas on their wings as they take to the air. Their soft monotonous cooing (which is paired in the Inca dove) has none of the slow cadence of a mourning dove's *oh–MEE—you—you—you* call.

Doves walk, rather than hop, along the ground as they feed. So do the horned larks which sometimes search for seeds and insects in the same fields, frequently arriving before worms exposed by a farmer's plow have had time to hide in the soil again. Horned larks are mostly light brown, with one black mark across the chest and another on each side of the head downcurving through the eye. On their head are two little backward-pointing black feathers they can raise like horns. In summer these larks migrate as far as northern Alaska and Baffin Land, but for the winter most of them come south into the United States and Mexico. Although they nest on the ground, they start early and may raise four broods before winter reduces the amount of food.

A recent immigrant to the New World, the cattle egret, shows even less hesitation about walking along the furrows right behind a tractor. Known as the buff-backed heron in the Old World, from which it spread under its own power in the 1950's, it shows buffy color in its head, chest, legs, and back feathers only during the breeding season. At other times, it is just an all-white egret with a yellow beak, red eyes, and dark legs. It accepts an agricultural machine as a fair substitute for the Cape buffaloes or elephants that its African cousins follow for the stirred-up insects left in their wake.

So far we have not seen a cattle egret on a suburban lawn, but two of the jay-sized woodpeckers often hop about in search of ants. Except in the Far North to the east of Alaska and west of the Rockies,

Yellow-Shafted Flicker
Colaptes auratus
Length 13″ to 14″

the woodpecker with this habit is the **yellow-shafted flicker,** named for the bright yellow below its wings and for its loud call—*FLICK-FLICK-FLICK*—in a long series. In the Gulf States the bird is often known as the yellowhammer. To the west of the Rockies, from Alaska into Mexico, the very similar **red-shafted flicker** takes its place, known by the orange-red beneath its wings and much of its tail. In both of these flickers, the throat bears a well-defined black collar mark, and the undersides are boldly speckled. The male flicker has a "mustache mark" extending in line with his beak, and his behavior shows that he relies upon recognizing another male by this feature, which is lacking on females and young birds. On a yellow-shafted flicker male the mustache is black, whereas that of the red-shafted is a rusty red.

Red-Shafted Flicker
Colaptes cafer
Length 12½" to 14"

North American Birds

One of the banded plovers—the **killdeer**—scurries along over some of the same fields as flickers, particularly during early spring migration. At that season, all killdeers are mature and their necks bear two black rings. Later in the year when the juvenile birds are flying with the adults, we see young killdeers with only one neck band. All call their name so loudly and persistently that they earn their species name—*vociferus*. From coast to coast, through settled Canada and all of the United States to the south, this bird tries to lead intruders away from its nest by acting as though one wing were broken. It winters as far south as northern Peru.

Killdeer
Charadrius vociferus
Length 9″ to 11″

Familiar Species

To two of our neighborly birds, the ground seems much too low down. Never have we seen the **common nighthawk** on the ground if it could find a tree branch or a flat rooftop to rest on. Never should you expect to see a chimney swift resting anywhere unless you can somehow manage to look down a big chimney with a flashlight after dark. Nighthawks flap erratically through the air, flashing the white near the tips of their long, angled, pointed wings, and capturing flying insects in a broad, wide-open mouth. The bird's harsh call PEENK comes down to us, often from a twilit sky, voiced as the bird makes a characteristic extra-quick flap with its wings, so that three beats come in rapid succession. Because nighthawks are often active, flying and calling and catching insects all night long, they are known in many parts of North America as "bull bats." It seems impossible to learn whether they capture their prey by accident, as though trawling the sky, or by vision or some other sense. Few birds are equipped for activity in such dim light.

Common Nighthawk
Chordeiles minor
Length 8½″ to 10″

Chimney Swift
Chaetura pelagica
Length 5″ to 5½″

Barn Owl
Tyto alba
Length 15″ to 20″

Chimney swifts twitter almost constantly as they wheel and dart. Each has a dark body shaped like a cigar and a neck so short that the head barely extends forward of the arc made by the outstretched wings. Toward dusk, all chimney swifts funnel downward quite suddenly into chimneys where they perch and nest—substitutes for the hollow trees that have grown so scarce. Both chimney swifts and nighthawks migrate to South America for the winter, the swifts to one small area of eastern Peru near the headwaters of the Amazon.

Night is mostly a time for owls, such as the sleek **barn owls**— sometimes called "monkey-faced owls"—who seek cavities in hollow trees and deserted buildings as a place to raise a family; and the **screech owls,** whose quavering song is no screech by any stretch of the imagination. Both are resident birds in southern Canada and all of the United States to the south, as well as Mexico and, in the case of the barn owl, some of the West Indies too. Allied races of the barn owl are found over much of southern Eurasia, making it one kind of bird that colonial naturalists recognized in the New World. Barn owls and screech owls are among the most useful of all birds in reducing the number of rats and mice around human communities. But how they catch crayfish and earthworms in the dark, as they do quite often, remains a mystery.

Screech Owl
Otus asio
Length 8" to 10"

These two kinds of owl are the largest of the predatory birds that will accept a nest box near people. Often at night they will approach a person who makes loud squeaky kissing noises on the wrist, in poor imitation of an overly vocal mouse. At close range, however, their big eyes and excellent hearing detect the difference. On broad wings that seem soundproofed, the owls vanish again into the dark to continue hunting genuine vermin in the community.

By day, some larger birds patrol the same regions for carcasses and edible wastes. We may question their tastes in food, but have to recognize their assistance in sanitation and their skill in the air. **Turkey vultures** flap their wings ponderously to gain altitude and then soar for hours, gliding from one updraft to the next. Their wings span as much as six feet and are held at a slight angle, like a wide-open V, each wing with a broad pale brown area along the trailing margin to the tip. The head of a young turkey vulture is gray but that of a mature adult is blood-red—enough like that of the domestic turkey to earn the descriptive name. Turkey vultures range far north in the Canadian prairies, but rarely visit northern New England; southward they are common into Central America and the West Indies, overlapping in some of their range with the black vulture of the tropical mainland—a slightly smaller bird with white wing tips that flaps more often between short glides in which it holds its wings level.

Most versatile of the scavengers is the **herring gull,** which can soar quite well despite its narrower wings and shorter span (no more than 56 inches). Formerly this, our largest gray-backed gull, patrolled mostly the coasts, the major rivers, and larger lakes. It sought out flotsam and jetsam, shelled marine animals it could drop and smash on rocks, and the eggs or young of smaller birds nesting in the open. But while still generally known as "the sea gull," it has now spread across all of North America—except for the arid and mountainous Midwest—as a patron of garbage dumps. It sometimes competes with black vultures for Southern garbage and, like them, never hesitates to seize, kill, and eat any obstreperous rat that runs within reach. So nourishing is America's refuse that the numbers of herring gulls are now vastly greater than at any time in the past. We see and hear them flying overhead, calling. Wherever they flock together, there is a mighty disciplined social order. Big old herring

Turkey Vulture
Cathartes aura
Length 29″; Wingspread 70″

Herring Gull
Larus argentatus
Length 23″ to 26″; Wingspread 54″ to 58″

gulls take precedence over two-year-olds with brown on the wings and across the tip of the tail. One-year-olds are sooty brown. Only the young of the year approach the adults with their white heads and tails, to peck at the orange mark near the tip of the lower bill by way of begging for food. All of these gesture are accompanied by calls of wondrous variety—clearly a language the gulls understand.

Herring gulls have spread on their own, but others of the birds that associate with mankind were brought to the New World deliberately. The rock dove of Mediterranean countries and rocky coasts of Ireland and Scotland came as the domesticated pigeon, only to spread, nesting on buildings from coast to coast and northern Canada deep into Latin America. In cities it is better known than any other bird.

Tying for a place as the second most familiar bird in urban areas are the **house sparrow,** actually a weaver finch native to Eurasia and Africa, and the **common starling,** widespread from the British Isles and northern Spain across the Old World to Siberia. The adaptability and aggressiveness of these two birds matches the character of furred immigrants like the brown rat, the black rat, and the house mouse. Yet unlike the rodents, which arrived by accident in infested ships, the birds were brought to America and liberated with what seemed the best of intentions. The sparrows were to free the trees of the New World of destructive cankerworms, and the starlings were to eat other harmful insects.

The sparrows, then known as English sparrows, were imported and freed at Brooklyn in 1850, and later at Halifax and Quebec. They spread to Newfoundland, Cuba, and Jamaica, deep into Mexico, to the Pacific coast, and northward into Canada's Northwest Territories. They ate some insects, but mainly turned to grain, fruit, seeds, manure, and garbage. They drove away native birds and produced messy nests in every urban cranny—often in the ivy covering older buildings. The starlings were released in New York City's Central Park in 1890 and 1891. They became pests around public buildings, raided orchards and grain fields, drove out more native birds, and spread north to Labrador and across Canada to the Rockies, and southwestward across all of the United States into Mexico. Admittedly they are colorful, remarkably varied in their calls, and skilled in mimicking other birds. They eat both harmful insects and

House Sparrow
Passer domesticus
Length 5″ to 6¼″

Starling
Sturnus vulgaris
Length 7½″ to 8½″

weed seeds as part of a versatile diet. But both of these introduced birds became so great a nuisance that Congress showed almost no reluctance in passing the Lacey Act of 1907, forbidding the introduction of any other warm-blooded creature, feathered or otherwise, before exhaustive tests were made to be sure that history would not repeat itself.

There is a limit to how close we want a bird to nest, and how much we want to hear its voice. We have to evict a robin if she builds in the pendant light fixture of an unscreened porch (the heat of the bulb might cook her eggs or start a fire). But most of our native birds value their privacy more than the robin does. In fact, nine-tenths of the continent's birds are so aloof it is man who must continually seek them out in their wide-flung habitats.

CHAPTER THREE

BIRDS IN THE FOREST

FOREST BIRDS AND LUMBERMEN REGARD TREES IN ENTIRELY DIFFERENT WAYS. To a bird, a tree offers shelter, nesting sites, and a wealth of insects and fruit, mostly among the topmost branches. The lumberman looks mainly at tree trunks, and knows that the boards cut from them will have fewer knots if there are no branches at all. To him, the crown of a tree—the twigs and leaves—is just so much waste slash. He ignores any forest whose trees are small and twisted. Shrubby undergrowth may be woody, but it yields no wood. Yet birds find a multitude of homes in trees that lack commercial quality, on land that would not be classified as bearing timber.

The northernmost forest of America provides for both birds and sawmills. It is an evergreen wonderland of spruces and fir, spread diagonally across the continent from New England to Alaska, from which the forester sees profits in the form of pulpwood and Christmas trees. On the north, this dark green belt gives way to bleak treeless tundra. Along its southern fringe, white pines are more numerous. There, too, deciduous trees appear: paper birch, hard maples, and gray-barked beech.

North American Birds

In the Appalachian Mountains and for many miles to the east and west of these ancient peaks, birds find remnants of a once-continuous forest. Oaks are plentiful, and various hickories thrive. Yellow poplar grows large. Yellow pine and red cedar contribute foods for feathered residents. Further south, this mixed forest gives way to stands of species that tolerate only mild frosts: magnolias, sweet gum, tupelo, southern oaks interspersed with fragrant pines, particularly the slash, the loblolly, and the longleaf. Lowland swamps thick with bald cypress offer a haven for both forest birds and waterfowl. West of these forests, from the Canadian border to the gulf coast of Texas, an open savanna studded with oaks grades northwestward into grassland, or southwestward into various kinds of desert scrub.

From the foothills of the Rocky Mountains across to the shores of the Pacific, variations in altitude become more important than latitude. Height above sea level alters the climate, converting the forest map into a patchwork of challenging complexity. The west coast proper has its giant Sitka spruces, Douglas firs, and coastal redwoods standing in great misty glades. Higher slopes are clad in western yellow (ponderosa) pine, sugar pine with its tremendous cones, and Engelmann spruce. These in turn give way to near-horizontal bands of quaking aspen, which turn gloriously golden in autumn—soon after most of the birds there have flown away, down-slope and southward.

Many birds prefer the borders of their forest, where they can move quickly and easily from the cool shadows of the trees into the open spaces beyond and enjoy the best of both. The handsome **red-tailed hawk** chooses a tall tree in a secluded grove for its high nest of sticks and branches. But it goes to the forest edge to perch motionless on an exposed limb and watch for rabbits. Or it will soar for hours over open country, its broad wings spread horizontally for as much as four feet from tip to tip, its tail often tilted at a slight angle but still showing uniformly pink, orange, or reddish, its eyes scanning the ground for a rodent it can catch with a single swoop.

A nest tree in a moist location, perhaps a dense swamp, appeals more to the similar but smaller red-shouldered hawk. It seldom perches anywhere else to show its distinctive reddish-brown shoulders. But the same color shows as a broad band in the forward

Red-Tailed Hawk
Buteo jamaicensis
Length 20½″ to 22″; Wingspread 48″ to 53″

North American Birds

portion of each outstretched wing as the bird soars above large culti-vated fields, searching for suitable prey. Like the still-smaller **broad-winged hawk,** which nests in the woodlands and hunts from a perch, the red-shouldered hawk wears curved dark bands on its tail, both below and above. The broad-winged's appetite matches its size. Often the hawk flashes away from its perch to capture a large grass-hopper or a small lizard—food with less appeal for the bigger birds. The broad-winged and red-shouldered are hawks of the eastern United States and adjacent Canada, whereas the red-tailed finds its nesting places and prey over most of the continent—from Alaska to the north shore of the St. Lawrence River and southward into the West Indies and Central America.

Broad-Winged Hawk
Buteo platypterus
Length 15″ to 17″; Wingspread 35″ to 37″

The hawks work out of the forest by day and the owls by night. Indeed, the range of the **great horned owl** is almost the same as that of the red-tailed hawk, except that this large owl rarely visits the West Indies. In arid areas of the American Southwest and Latin America, it finds perches for the day in isolated trees far from dense forest. The great horned owl prefers rabbits and rats as food, but occasionally kills and eats a skunk—apparently unable to smell or taste the powerful repellent the skunk uses in self-defense.

Great Horned Owl
Bubo virginianus
Length 20″ to 23″

Long-Eared Owl
Asio otus
Length 13″ to 16″

The **long-eared owl** is only about two-thirds the size of the great horned, although its wings are proportionately longer. While resting, it ordinarily sits in an evergreen on a limb close to the trunk of the tree, and holds its body feathers close making itself appear tall and very slim. Usually it nests in a conifer, too, but never so far north as does the great horned owl. In the Old World, the long-eared owl has a similar distribution, ranging south to the Mediterranean but north only into southern Scandinavia.

We are so used to seeing owls illustrated with large yellow eyes that to find ones with dark brown eyes seems strange. Yet this is the natural eye color of the large barred owl, which makes its home in the wettest swampy forests it can find east of the Rockies, and of the little **flammulated owl** which inhabits western pine woods from Canada to Mexico. The flammulated has tiny ear tufts, but the barred owl is said to be "earless," meaning only that it lacks the distinctive feathers that project so prominently from the heads of the great horned and other big-eared owls. "Earless" owls hear magnificently, and use this ability in conjunction with their keen vision to locate prey in dark places.

Flammulated Owl
Otus flammeolus
Length 6" to 7"

Saw-Whet Owl
Aegolius acadicus
Length 7″ to 8½″

Birds In The Forest

Of the earless little owls with golden eyes, the most widespread is the **saw-whet.** Found coast to coast across southern Canada, it also nests in the northern United States and winters well to the south. But it is so strictly nocturnal, hiding in dense evergreens and swampy thickets by day, that it seems rarer than is actually the case. Anyone who camps in the saw-whet's favorite haunts in summer is likely to hear its ventriloquial call—a series of short whistles that might suggest the sound made by a man filing the teeth of a saw. West of the Rockies, the range of the saw-whet overlaps with that of the still smaller **pygmy owl,** which often flies around by day, catching insects and mice. The pygmy nests in the woodlands but hunts in the open. Its tail is longer than that of most owls, and its flight follows an undulating course like that of a shrike.

Pygmy Owl
Glaucidium gnoma
Length 7″ to 7½″

North American Birds

This peculiar style of flight is a family trait among the wood-peckers. They beat their wings rapidly to gain altitude and begin a power dive; then they coast, often with wings partly closed, conserving momentum, only to flare their wings again and rise at the expense of speed. Hurtling along in this fashion, they can continue mile after mile. Except for the sapsuckers, few go far, because their food and shelter are available almost equally in all seasons and they need not migrate to get it. The sapsuckers, however, feed on tree sap and the small insects that are attracted to it; the birds get their nourishment by drilling parallel rows of small shallow pits in live trees and returning to drink after the sap has collected. Occasionally sapsuckers fail to visit their drinking sites often enough during warm weather, and the sap ferments. Then they and some other birds that drink from sapsucker holes, get tipsy and have difficulty alighting where they want to. Over much of North America, the yellow-bellied sapsucker shows this habit. In the West at higher elevations and more northern states in summer, Williamson's sapsucker stays

Downy Woodpecker
Dendrocopos pubescens
Length 6½″ to 7″

mostly in pine forests. In both kinds, only the male has red and broad black markings on the head; females are brown in the corresponding areas, and on the back as well.

Most of our woodpeckers show this same color difference: males have a patch of red on the head, females and juveniles, none. No doubt these birds can tell at a glance, just as we can. We notice this distinction when the little **downy woodpeckers** come to our feeders for a snack of suet, or when the big hairy woodpeckers arrive, each almost half again as big as a downy and surely more than twice the weight. These two are the most widespread of North American woodpeckers, nesting in orchards and mixed woodlands, drilling and pecking into bark for insects that are attacking the trees.

The sound of a downy woodpecker hammering at a tree often has the high speed and regularity of a typewriter underlining a word. A hairy is noticeably slower and louder at close range. Both birds make roughly circular, conical cavities. But the big **pileated woodpecker,** now uncommon but widespread in eastern North America

Pileated Woodpecker
Dryocopus pileatus
Length 17″ to 19½″

and some parts of the Northwest, sounds like a woodsman cutting down a tree. Often it opens roughly rectangular cavities three inches wide and a foot or more in length, reaching deep into the dead wood of an old tree to get at the insects boring within. With its all-black body and giant size, the pileated might be mistaken for a crow except for its white marks on head, neck, and underwings, and its high pointed crest—flame red in the male, and mostly black in its mate. The rare ivory-billed woodpecker, last reported in one swamp forest of eastern Texas, is a similar bird of even larger size, with white on the back and wing tips and black on the front of the crest.

Observers are often so impressed by the way a woodpecker clings to the bark, propping itself firmly by means of sharp-tipped tail feathers, and hammering into solid wood without inflicting brain concussion upon itself, that the vegetable part of its normal diet goes unnoticed. Actually a great many of the smaller woodpeckers get more than half their diet in the form of fruits, seeds, and the crumbs of nutritious cambium they swallow when digging through the inner bark for insect borers. The ladder-backed woodpecker that drills into mesquite trees in the American Southwest and Mexico is often called the "cactus woodpecker" because it eats so many cactus fruits, apparently avoiding the spines and bristles. The acorn woodpecker of live oak woodlands in California and from New Mexico south into highlands of Central America, has earned a bad reputation with telephone linesmen by excavating thousands of holes in the company's poles to hold individual acorns—stored against a future time of need. Each acorn is hammered in place without breaking the shell. As many as 1500 may be imbedded in a single pole.

The **red-headed woodpecker** of deciduous woodlands east of the Rocky Mountains favors acorns too, but turns to corn, grapes, and many other cultivated fruits as they ripen. Fortunately for the agriculturalist, these handsome birds are not too numerous and do eat large numbers of May beetles, grasshoppers, and insect pests, even hawking them out of the air like flycatchers. The red of their head and neck contrasts sharply with the dark blue of the back and wing tips, the white of the chest and rump, and the trailing edges of the wings. Both sexes of the red-headed are colored alike, but the young have brown where the adults are red and blue.

Red-Headed Woodpecker
Melanerpes erythrocephalmus
Length 8½" to 9½"

Lewis' Woodpecker
Asyndesmus lewis
Length 10½″ to 11½″

Birds In The Forest

In the western United States and northern Mexico, we encounter **Lewis' woodpecker,** with similar feeding habits. In autumn it becomes gregarious before migrating toward the southern extremities of its range. It is then that we notice how unwoodpeckerlike this bird can be. Although catching an occasional insect on the wing, Lewis' woodpecker specializes on fruits. It alights crosswise on branches of trees, instead of clinging head up to the bark. And it flaps along at a steady pace, instead of showing the exuberant undulations of its relatives. That it is a dark green bird with a red face and rosy underparts only makes it more distinctive.

Among the orthodox woodpeckers, there are a good many look-alikes and act-alikes. Yet all manage to avoid serious competition with each other, mostly by choosing different food, places to nest, and times to be in each part of the continent. Sometimes the change comes unexpectedly within just a few miles' travel. You can drive south from Minnesota or west from any part of the Atlantic coast from Delaware to Florida and stay in the territory of the **red-bellied woodpecker** for hundreds of miles. But if you cross Texas southwest-

Red-Bellied Woodpecker
Centurus carolinus
Length 9″ to 10½″

North American Birds

ward, you pass abruptly into the territory of the **golden-fronted woodpecker,** which extends into Mexico. These look-alikes and act-alikes even sound alike. But the red-bellied has red on the back of the neck in both sexes where the golden-fronted is golden orange. The female golden-fronted wears no red at all, whereas the female red-bellied differs from her mate mostly in having a brownish-gray cap instead of his all-red hood. To us, the most puzzling thing about these similar birds is why they are named as they are, since neither is conspicuously more red-bellied nor golden-fronted than the other!

Golden-Fronted Woodpecker
Centurus aurifrons
Length 8½″ to 10½″

The **whip-poor-will** and the **poor-will** seem to divide the continent between them; the poor-will in the West and the whip-poor-will to the east and from along the Mexican border southward. The whip-poor-will hawks for its food much as the common nighthawk does, whereas the poor-will catches most of the insects it eats by making short hops from the ground. Seemingly, when the whip-poor-wills migrate to Florida and Mexico for the winter, the poor-wills cling to some canyon wall and become torpid—living on their fat with lowered body temperature—as no other bird is known to do. These

Whip-Poor-Will
Caprimulgus vociferus
Length 9″ to 10″

North American Birds

differences in habit and distribution could never be guessed from holding a whip-poor-will in one hand and a poor-will in the other. The whip-poor-will would be larger and have more white on the back corners of its tail. Its voice is louder and a syllable longer, and it often calls endlessly. But these birds of the forest, which more people hear than see, have inherited real dissimilarities their sizes and feathers do not reveal.

Poor-Will
Phalaenoptilus nuttallii
Length 7″ to 8½″

Birds In The Forest

The 100th parallel of longitude divides the **eastern wood pewee** from the western wood pewee all summer. Just a few miles westward will take us from a woodland where the pewee calls PEE-a-WEEE (ending as high as it began) and plaintively PEE-wee (descending in pitch at the conclusion), to one where the song is more uniformly PEE-errr, with a burr at the end. Both are inconspicuous flycatchers of the shadows, in deciduous and coniferous woods, building exquisite saucer-shaped nests on horizontal limbs and camouflaging their structures with lichens.

Eastern Wood Pewee
Contopus virens
Length 6″ to 6½″

North American Birds

The **great crested flycatcher** is a distinctly larger bird, the only one of its kind with a reddish tail to be found nesting east of the 100th parallel. It is an aggressive denizen of the tree tops in deciduous and mixed woodlands from southern Alberta to Nova Scotia, south to Florida and eastern Texas. Often it decorates its nest cavity with a shed snakeskin, finding a new place to rear its young each spring when it returns from winter quarters in Cuba, Southern Mexico and Central America.

Great-Crested Flycatcher
Myiarchus crinitus
Length 8″ to 9″

Birds In The Forest

Sometimes the pattern of bird distribution in the forests matches the types of trees. This is a feature the various jays appear to heed, even if their audacity shows no other bounds. Just as the northern coniferous forest extends from coast to coast, descending southward in the West, so too the **gray jay** follows this pattern and learns to gain from the presence of lumberjacks—sharing their possessions to the point where they name it the "Camp robber" and "Whiskey Jack." South of this territory and east of the Rockies, among mixed

Gray Jay
Perisoreus canadensis
Length 10" to 13"

Steller's Jay
Cyanocitta stelleri
Length 12″ to 13⅓″

Pinyon Jay
Gymnorhinus cyanocephala
Length 9″ to 11¾″

woods of pine and oaks, the handsome, raucous blue jay makes its home. It is the only crested bird of this kind in two-thirds of North America. West of the mountains, particularly in coniferous forests that do not suit a gray jay, the crested **Steller's jay** takes the place of the blue jay, even to chasing crows and harassing owls whenever possible. In more arid regions of the West, the steel-blue **pinyon jay** chooses nest sites in the pinyon pines, but often feeds on the ground among the shrubby sagebrush. Only a detailed map showing the vegetation can indicate how the pinyon jay avoids overlap with the **scrub jay,** a remarkably secretive bird that haunts the scrub oaks and that finds a suitable place to live in much of Florida.

Scrub Jay
Aphelocoma coerulescens
Length 11″ to 13″

Turkey
Meleagris gallopavo
Length 36″ to 48″

Birds In The Forest

Back in the days when the woodlands of North America were safer for **turkeys,** they were far more numerous than they are today. Yet their scattered modern distribution, from southern New England into Mexico, from Florida to coastal California and Idaho, shows the number of different forest types in which they could find enough to eat. Depending upon the season and place, they still choose a wide assortment of hard fruits, seeds, and insects, changing their diet considerably as they grow from small poults to full-sized hens and gobblers. Through much of this range, although not in the far north, they overlap with the **ruffed grouse,** whose 29 ounces seems heavy to a sportsman who has not had the experience of getting a 36-pound turkey. Ruffed grouse chicks start life at a much smaller size and, although they are protected by the hen, they choose their own food (to match their size) right from the beginning. Month for month,

Ruffed Grouse
Bonasa umbellus
Length 16″ to 19″

North American Birds

they are always smaller than the turkeys and find food the larger birds would automatically ignore. In addition, the grouse feed more on buds, green leaves, and fleshy fruits, which makes them less dependent on finding beechnuts and acorns—foods on which turkeys fatten and grow large. Conflicts do not develop, despite the fact that neither bird travels appreciably during the year; neither inherits a migratory behavior.

Perhaps it is sheer coincidence that the turkey gobbler, when displaying before a hen, spreads his tail fan in a fashion similar to the ruffed grouse cock. He drags his wing tips stiffly against the ground, rattling them vigorously. The grouse chooses a hollow log as a resonator to stand on while beating his shorter wings—drumming his feathers against the wood about forty times a second. The turkey has no feathers on his neck to spread, but its bright red color and pendant wattle are the counterpart of the ruff the ruffed grouse raises to make him appear larger.

Sometimes we wonder whether it is the shelter of the forests and orchards or the big hairy caterpillars to be found there that attract North American cuckoos to these areas. **Yellow-billed cuckoos** winter

Yellow-Billed Cuckoo
Coccyzus americanus
Length 11″ to 12½″

in all parts of South America except the arid west coast, and come to build their frail nests and feed on such insects as tent caterpillars in most of the United States and southeastern Canada. Black-billed cuckoos, which winter in northwestern South America, have a smaller and more northern nesting range but seem to choose the same kinds of nest sites, build comparable nests, and hunt for similar food. Farmers generally welcome these birds because of their effectiveness in reducing the number of insect pests, and claim that they are "rain crows" whose repetitious calls foretell a thundershower.

Judged on the basis of body weight, it appears only reasonable that a six-inch titmouse weighing a quarter as much as a twelve-inch cuckoo should seek somewhat smaller prey than two-inch caterpillars. But actually the sharp-eyed little titmice, digging into bark crevices and scouting over leaf and twig surfaces, go for far smaller fare. They eat bark beetles an eighth of an inch in length and (during the winter) countless plant lice eggs, each of which is less than a fiftieth of an inch in diameter. Policing the trees in the southeastern half of the United States is the **tufted titmouse,** which calls *PEter, PEter, PEter,* and often associates with its close kin, the chickadee. West Virginians have chosen it as their state bird.

Tufted Titmouse
Parus bicolor
Length 6" to 6½"

North American Birds

Acrobatic as titmice and chickadees are, they never seem to ignore gravity as deliberately as a nuthatch can. Over much of the United States and southern Canada, the **white-breasted nuthatch** forages, chiefly in the deciduous forests. Like the tufted titmouse, it finds little need to migrate. In winter, it merely increases the proportion of seeds in its diet and takes turns with chickadees, grosbeaks, finches, and jays in raiding bird feeders for sunflower seeds. Provident nuthatches hammer extra seeds into bark crevices, where they can be found even after ice storms have locked away all other food.

When a nuthatch calls *INK INK INK* instead of *YANK YANK*, we can be almost certain that it is the red-breasted nuthatch instead of the white-breasted. This bird also comes for a handout when the food is scarce in coniferous forests. Otherwise it spreads far north in summer to Newfoundland and southern Alaska, and to the southern states in winter. It has a black line through the eye that divides the white on the face, as well as a brownish underside. In the West, its range overlaps with that of the smaller pygmy nuthatch, whose

White-Breasted Nuthatch
Sitta carolinensis
Length 5″ to 6″

gray cap comes down to its black eye. But the pygmy spends only the cold months at low elevations; for nesting and food for its young, it flies to the mountain pinelands and shows a special preference for groves of ponderosa—the western yellow pine.

Crevices in tree bark hide the insects brown creepers hunt. These inconspicuous brown birds always alight head-up on the tree trunk and use their long, stiff tail feathers as a prop, much as a woodpecker does. But they probe for food, with a down-curved slender beak, never pecking deeper than the natural crevices allow. Their thin drawn-out song is so high-pitched that some people cannot hear it even at close range.

No one has difficulty hearing the songs and calls of the small brown wrens of the forest, for they are loud and clear. Largest of the wrens in the eastern half of the continent is the **Carolina wren.** Its most frequent song can be imitated by saying *tea-kettle* repeatedly at half-second intervals. But the bird varies its sounds, imitating unrelated neighbors so often that for years the Carolina wren was

Carolina Wren
Thryothorus ludovicianus
Length 5½″ to 6″

called the "mocking wren." It is almost as characteristic of the South as the mockingbird, and rarely visits New England. In moister forests and underbrush, the more migratory **winter wren** hunts for insects in a similar way. It is a tiny bird with the shortest tail of any wren and brown markings underneath. It produces a loud rippling melody both in its nesting territories across most of Canada, south along the Appalachians, and north near the Pacific coast to Alaska, and in its wintering grounds farther south. It is the only wren in Europe and much of Asia, and consequently is the one most referred to in Western literature.

During the winter, the southern and Pacific states are visited regularly by kinglets, wren-sized birds that seem extraordinarily trusting except while nesting. Then they are exquisitely secretive, sometimes abandoning a nest they believe to have been discovered. Nesting in coniferous forests, they go to great effort to suspend their delicate structure, weaving leaves, bark, moss, and other plant materials into the form of a globe held together with spider web, and lined with hair or feathers. Both sexes of the **ruby-crowned kinglet** have a conspicuous white eye ring, but only the male has a narrow streak of brilliant red feathers which show like a bloody mark atop his head when he is excited. The ruby-crowned has a loud, ringing central movement to its song, very different from the high-pitched *ZEE-ZEE-ZEE* of the golden-crowned kinglet. Both sexes of the golden-crowned have a conspicuous yellow stripe atop the head, that of the male additionally bright with an orange center line.

The kinglets of America are woodland birds in a technical sense; they are "sylvan," members of the family Sylviidae. In the New World this family has few representatives, but in the Old World most of its widely known, different kinds are called warblers. "Warblers" in America do not warble and belong to a different family (the Parulidae), often distinguished as the wood warblers. Smaller than most sparrows, every one of them is an insect-eater, dodging among the foliage of shrubbery and trees in search of food. Of all the birds that migrate, they are the most tantalizing. The bird-watcher gets only glimpses of their plumage and snatches of their songs as challenges to recognition. In late summer, moreover, many warblers replace the bright patterns of plumage worn on the northward mating and nesting trip with different, duller colors, more like those of juveniles—which are also present among southbound flocks.

Winter Wren
Troglodytes troglodytes
Length 4″ to 4½″

Ruby-Crowned Kinglet
Regulus calendula
Length 3¾″ to 4½″

North American Birds

In the successive waves that fly north each spring usually the first warbler to arrive is the **black-and-white.** It acts like a nuthatch, alighting in any position on the bark and branches of trees, selecting plant lice, click beetles, and many other kinds of crawling insects. The bird has come from its winter quarters in the Gulf States, the northern West Indian islands, and Latin America as far south as Ecuador. Feeding by day and flying onward at night, it heads for some individual destination in a northern woodland where it will nest on the ground near the foot of a tree. Some stop short in Georgia and eastern Texas; others go on to the Yukon and Newfoundland. To human eyes, the choice of a nesting site seems arbitrary, perhaps because we do not yet understand the values each bird finds in its world.

Black-and-White Warbler
Mniotilta varia
Length 5″ to 5½″

Myrtle warblers sweep through most of the United States, heading for nesting sites from northern New England across Canada to Alaska. Migrating from their winter territories in the southern United or Latin America as far south as Panama, they mix with other warblers, chickadees, and kinglets, hunting for insects at any level among the expanding foliage. They will select their nesting sites in a forest, not far from the spot where they themselves hatched out, and will build nests like their parents did—on a conifer, between 30 and 40 feet above the ground.

Myrtle Warbler
Dendroica coronata
Length 5″ to 6″

Audubon's Warbler
Dendroica auduboni
Length 5″ to 5½″

Prairie Warbler
Dendroica discolor
Length 4½″ to 5″

The myrtle warbler has a white chin patch and yellow cap, as well as a yellow rump and white on the sides of its tail. Its western counterpart is **Audubon's warbler,** which has a yellow chin and a solid patch of white on the wings instead of two white wing bars. In the East, we might confuse the myrtle with the magnolia warbler, which has the solid white wing patch, yellow rump, and white on the tail, but a steel-blue cap and black streaks on a yellow breast. A magnolia can be flying with the myrtles, heading for much the same forest location, but builds its nest and does its summer foraging at a lower level—between three and 35 feet above the ground. The name "magnolia" for this bird merely shows that the first specimen known to science was the one Alexander Wilson shot and described. It was on migration, temporarily hunting insects in a magnolia tree.

Similarly, the **prairie warbler** has nothing to do with prairies. It is a bird of scrub oak and second-growth pine woods anywhere in the eastern United States. Building its nest in the top of some low bush, it forages low down, eating insects almost exclusively, but also darts upward to catch gnats and moths on the wing. Distinctively, it often wags its tail while perched, for no known reason. Often a pair of prairie warblers get their young airborne and head south by July, progressing toward winter territory in southern Florida, the Bahamas, and the northernmost West Indies. By then, their wings are barred in dull yellow, not white; the rust colored streaks on the back of the adult male have gone; even the lines of black spots on the sides of the body are faint. But all members of the brood are still wagging their tails and occasionally pursuing an insect on the wing—antics that few warblers show.

The nesting sites chosen by warblers are generally as distinctive as the males' bright mating plumage. While incubating their eggs and feeding their young, moreover, they tend to forage for insects at the same altitude at which they build their nests. Black-and-whites break the rule by foraging on the bark of trees and nesting on the ground, as do the Canada warblers. Sometimes, we suspect, the Canadas frighten their prey into flight by scurrying around among the low bushes of their hunting territory.

The chestnut-sided warblers nest in low bushes and pick insects off the foliage at that level. After their northward migration ends, somewhere in the northeastern United States and adjacent Canada,

North American Birds

their territory overlaps slightly with that of the magnolia warblers that forage a bit higher up. Myrtles occupy the next stratum toward the forest canopy, coast to coast from Alaska to Labrador.

In the high forests of the West, **Townsend's warblers** nest in the treetops. In the East, their counterparts are the Blackburnians. The distinctive males draw attention to themselves with high-pitched songs, which those upon the ground can hear coming from the crowns of the trees. Each male Blackburnian warbler has orange markings on his head, a clear orange chest and cap, but white underparts sparingly marked with black. Townsend's has a black throat and cap, and coarse black marks only in the yellow portions of his underparts. The females and young are much more alike, as are the males when on southbound migration and during winter. Often only a hint remains of the dark spotting on the throat of Towsend's, lacking entirely in any Blackburnian. So slight are the clues by which we know one warbler from the other. Yet their inner heritage leaves no chance for confusion since these birds sort themselves out geographically and vertically to mate and nest in the coniferous forests.

Townsend's Warbler
Dendroica townsendi
Length 4½″ to 5″

Not all of the 109 different kinds of insect-eating wood warblers in America are so small and dart about so actively. The **ovenbird** is almost thrush-like and walks along the ground eating insects, spiders, snails, slugs, earthworms, and other small creatures. On its northward migration from Florida and tropical America, and on its nesting grounds from Oklahoma and Virginia northward to Alberta and Newfoundland, it attracts attention with a distinctive call that gets louder as it progresses: *teacher*, TEACHER, *TEACHER*. Its nest is a lovely thing in the form of a Dutch oven with a doorway at one side, built out of grasses and bits of moss on the ground, usually at the foot of a tree.

Ovenbird
Seiurus aurocapillus
Length 5½″ to 6½″

North American Birds

The **yellow-breasted chat** is the largest of the warblers, between six and seven inches long—stouter than a catbird, but with a shorter tail. Its bright yellow throat, and olive back, wings, and tail are set off by white spectacles. The bird makes itself conspicuous with a most amazing song—a medley of clucking, mewing, gurgling, and whistled calls that sometimes is continued after dark. The relatively heavy beak handles a diet that includes considerable amounts of fruits and seeds as well as insects. Chats nest in most of the United States and northwestern Mexico, moving to the Tropics but not the West Indies for the winter.

Yellow-Breasted Chat
Icteria virens
Length 6½″ to 7½″

Birds In The Forest

It is much easier to credit redstarts with belonging to the warbler clan, even though their colors resemble those of orioles. The **American redstart** male is a flashing little bird, white below and on the legs, with orange patches on wings and tail that contrast sharply with black feathers elsewhere. Particularly on northward migration from the West Indies and Latin America toward deciduous forests between Florida and Newfoundland and western Canada, he chases after females traveling with him—as well as after the insects on which both sexes feed. Females also flash lemon-yellow patches on wings and tail, but are otherwise white below, gray on the head, and olive-green elsewhere. They build beautiful little nests in the understory of the forest. Each is suspended from an upright crotch, woven of fine plant materials to form a strong, thin-walled cup. Similar behavior is shown by the painted redstart, which crosses out of Mexico into the Arizona-Sonoran desert and seeks out canyons with scrub oak woodlands. But the painted male has no monopoly on his markings; they also appear on his mate and fledglings.

American Redstart
Setophaga ruticilla
Length 4½″ to 5½″

North American Birds

The vireos too suspend their nests from a crotch in a branch and rely upon the caterpillars and other insects they can glean from the foliage. But they are slower-moving birds. They usually blend so well with their surroundings that, although you can hear and recognize their loud songs, you may have to hunt for quite a while to find the singer. The **red-eyed vireo** may well be the most common bird in the deciduous forests east of the Rockies; its range extends far north into western Canada and to the Pacific coast. Often its song sounds like a robin hurrying through its repertoire, with pauses like syncopation in the phrasing. The bird itself lacks wing bars and distinctive marks except for a white stripe just above the eye; only adults have red eyes and a gray cap. Similarly, the white-eyed vireo, which generally chooses wetter parts of the woodland, is white-eyed only as an adult. Its call, white wing bars, and bright yellowish sides distinguish it from other olive-backed birds in the eastern United States. Both the red-eyed and the white-eyed vireos are considerably larger than the plain little **Hutton's vireos** of the Pacific coast and Mexico—birds that seek out groves of evergreen oaks.

Remembering the rule for vireos—that they have either a white stripe above the eye and no wing bars, or white wing bars and no stripe above the eye—we were once greatly puzzled to see a large long-tailed bird in a California pine forest whose song and shyness suggested a vireo—but with no wing bars and no stripe either. Instead, the sides of its tail were white. It proved to be **Townsend's solitaire,** a member of the thrush family found all the way from Mexico to Alaska in coniferous forests. Unlike a thrush, it perched on a sunny branch to sing and produced a loud warbling note. Its young have mottled chests, not the freckling worn by most juveniles of thrushes.

Red-Eyed Vireo
Vireo olivaceus
Length 5½″ to 6½″

Hutton's Vireo
Vireo huttoni
Length 4¼″ to 4¾″

Townsend's Solitaire
Myadestes townsendi
Length 8″ to 9½″

North American Birds

Only in winter do Pacific coast pine forests harbor **varied thrushes,** which migrate north to nest in moister groves of evergreens up through the Rockies and British Columbia to Alaska. The silhouette, size, and general coloration of the male varied suggest a robin with a black chest band. But his song consists of a long quavering whistle on a single note, followed (after an interval) by others in different keys. Only the young varied have freckled chests.

Varied Thrush
Ixoreus naevius
Length 9″ to 10″

We are far more used to the lovely harmonies produced by thrushes that retain their speckles for life. The flute-like arpeggios of the **hermit thrush** are heard all over its nesting range which extends from Massachusetts to Labrador, Alaska to Mexico. The delightful melody may die away briefly while the first brood of young are gaining their independence. Then the songs pick up again as the parents nest a second (and sometimes a third) time the same summer. Hermits rarely go far south for winter. The southern United States and Mexico are usually far enough.

Hermit Thrush
Hylocichla guttata
Length 6½″ to 7½″

North American Birds

The **veery** has the most subdued breast spots as an adult and sings flute-like notes rapidly descending the musical scale. It is a bird of moist deciduous forests almost all the way west across Canada and the northern United States from the east coast. Swainson's thrush (which formerly was called the olive-backed) sings an ascending scale, its notes having a rolling quality that some people say are "in spirals." Swainsons nest in the evergreen forests from Labrador to Alaska, and south in the West to almost the full length of California. Both Swainson's thrush and the veery journey a long way into South America each autumn. So does the **wood thrush,** whose round breast spots are the boldest of all. The wood thrush nests in the eastern United States and southern Ontario, all the way south to the Gulf of Mexico. Its beautiful markings, confiding ways, and exquisite whistling earned its election as the state bird of the District of Columbia. Its vocal phrases are spaced out with great deliberation—the fourth in each series usually ending with a quick downward trill. Only the nightingales of Europe and western Asia and the white-rumped chama thrush of India to the East Indies can rival the spotted thrushes of America for sweet fullness of song.

Veery
Hylocichla fuscescens
Length 6½" to 7½"

Wood Thrush
Hylocichla mustelina
Length 7½″ to 8½″

North American Birds

Probably it is a measure of human inability to follow and remember the high-speed inflections in many bird songs that leads us to compare so many to the carolling of the familiar robin. Not until technology managed to record bird sounds on magnetic tape and then play them back again at slower speed, was it possible to discover that the "wild and tinkling melody" of the little winter wren consists of exactly 130 notes in definite order, sung in 7.2 seconds. Even the larger Carolina wren, which varies its tune and so often mimics other birds, sings far faster than the best human whistler.

For songs that people regard as similar to a robin's, there are still a wealth of adjectives to suggest the differences. We describe the melody of the **scarlet tanager** as being more nasal, less ringing—like

Scarlet Tanager
Piranga olivacea
Length 6½" to 7½"

a robin with a head cold. Rather than try to imitate it, we listen instead for the distinctive *CHIP-churr* call of this tanager. *CHIP-churr* becomes a signal to start looking for a crestless scarlet bird with black wings and tail and a white beak; this is the male. His usually silent mate has a greenish beak, a greenish-yellow body, and even a greenish cast to her black wings and tail. After his fall moult, he resembles her except for the color of his beak, which remains unchanged.

Tanagers, with their family resemblance in calls, seem to have divided up North America fairly well. The scarlet stays in the East, nesting mostly north of the Mason-Dixon line. The **summer tanager**

Summer Tanager
Piranga rubra
Length 7″ to 7½″

Hepatic Tanager
Piranga flava
Length 7″ to 7¾″

Western Tanager
Piranga ludoviciana
Length 6¼″ to 7½″

spreads across the South; the **hepatic tanager** of Mexico comes across the border into canyons of Arizona and New Mexico. And the **western tanager** ranges northward in the West, almost to the Yukon. The summer tanager resembles a scarlet, but without contrasting black on wings or tail. The voice is like that of a healthy robin. The hepatic, a slightly larger bird, has a black beak, a hoarse song resembling that of the scarlet tanager, and a shadow under the eye of the male during the breeding season. Western tanagers are gaudy birds, with two white wing bars on their black wings; the tail is all black. The male's head is red, grading into bright yellow elsewhere on his body. He too sounds like a robin with a slight cold.

A different song—still like a robin's but more varied and richer, as though the robin had taken singing lessons—comes from other handsome vocalists of American forests. In the West south of the Canadian border, the singer is likely to be the **black-headed grosbeak;** in much of the rest of the continent, from northern British Columbia to Nova Scotia and the wooded mountains of Georgia, it is almost sure to be the rose-breasted grosbeak. Males of both species are black-headed and have white wing bars as well as white below the tail. They perch to sing on a high branch while their mates build characteristically loose nests in the forest understory. The females resemble large sparrows with streaked breasts and backs, but show their kinship to the grosbeak males by shelling sunflower seeds expertly with their huge beaks. (*Grosbeak* comes from the French *gros bec*, or "fat bill." The male black-headed grosbeak is largely a golden bird. He, his mate, and the female rose-breasteds all show gold below the wings when they fly. The male rose-breasted has a flush of red below his wings, but earns his name with his bright rose bib.

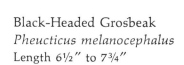

Black-Headed Grosbeak
Pheucticus melanocephalus
Length 6½" to 7¾"

North American Birds

In the spring and fall of each year, about the time the first of these grosbeaks arrive on migration, the large sparrow-like birds you are likely to see scratching on the ground are indeed sparrows—**fox sparrows.** They work like towhees, kicking the fallen leaves aside with both feet at once. But the males seldom sing until they are close to their breeding territory north of the Great Lakes across Canada, or southward in the West to northern Colorado and northern California. Fox sparrows winter in the southern United States.

When fox sparrows and grosbeaks arrive from the South, the spring migration has reached its peak. But when **pine grosbeaks** appear, both summer and autumn are past and winter is just around the corner. The beak of a pine grosbeak is hardly extraordinary; in fact, the bird resembles an overgrown purple finch—but one with white wing bars, which purple finches lack. Pine grosbeaks, too, rarely sing until they have returned to their nesting grounds in taiga country, and there they sound like robins. It is only when the snow gets too deep and the cold too bitter in the higher spruce forests of the West and Far North that they take refuge among the trees at temperate latitudes and lower altitudes.

Fox Sparrow
Passerella iliaca
Length 6¼″ to 7¼″

Pine Grosbeak
Pinicola enucleator
Length 8″ to 10″

North American Birds

These same conditions in the taiga bring us smaller birds in early winter, particularly the **pine siskins** and the **red crossbills.** The siskins arrive in flocks—each bird with a sharp-pointed beak, brown streaks on back and breast, and yellow on wings and base of tail. Like acrobats, they explore bare branches and twig tips for dormant insects and insect eggs that chickadees have overlooked. The crossbills explore the cones of pines and other conifers, and use their strangely crossed bill tips to extract the edible seeds. Although food is available to them all year (because the cones mature so slowly),

Pine Siskin
Spinus pinus
Length 4½″ to 5¼″

Red Crossbill
Loxia curvirostra
Length 5¼″ to 6½″

crossbills are wanderers. In winter they explore farther south and nearer to sea level, without following a predictable migratory schedule. But when the black, gray, white of the snowy forest is only echoed by the monochromatic plumage of the juncos and chickadees, the brick-red color of the male crossbill is a welcome change. His mate and young birds are olive-gray, their wings and tail dark gray, their rump and breast a yellow shade.

For people who live in the southern United States, winter is the season to enjoy the frequent songs and active company of handsome sparrows that nest far to the north. The **white-crowned sparrow** comes from nesting sites among the stunted shrubs of northern territories from Alaska to Labrador, and down the high forests of the West. It stays in the open where it can see in all directions, but generally in winter it seeks out the margins of a forest for trees to afford shelter should the weather worsen. Its clear whistles follow several patterns, but draw attention to the singer with its white streaked

White-Crowned Sparrow
Zonotrichia atricapilla
Length 6″ to 7″

North American Birds

head and pearly gray breast. The **white-throated sparrow,** despite the mark that gives it its name and a yellow spot between eye and beak, is far less noticeable for its appearance than for its clear high sweet whistle—two prolonged notes, followed by three more broken into three syllables each. We miss this music in the Far West and farthest north. It is a solo from the woodland sanctuary, a sonata from a free bird in the bush which, to us, is worth two in the hand.

White-Throated Sparrow
Zonotrichia albicollis
Length 6½″ to 7″

CHAPTER FOUR

OVER THE GRASSLANDS

Many millions of years before the world developed either grasses or prairies, birds found a place for themselves on the continents. Back in Mesozoic times, as feathered, warm-blooded animals evolved from their scaly, cold-blooded reptilian ancestors, they may also have begun their distinctive patterns of nest-building and regular migrations to places where food was seasonally plentiful. Freedom of movement to match regular changes in the weather is one great advantage to a creature capable of flight. And during the Eocene, when the new grasses evolved and began spreading over the summer-arid areas of the continents, they provided vast feeding areas for those with wings to reach them.

In North America, grasslands as we know them have a short history. They developed in the continent's heartland less than fifteen thousand years ago, after a warming climate caused the great glaciers to melt. Freed of ice that had spread as far south as Cape Cod, Long Island, and St. Louis, Missouri, the land drained off in new river patterns. Vegetation slowly spread northward and up the mountains, according to inherited tolerances and opportunity. Prior to this enormous change, we can only suspect that grasslands existed closer to

135

the Equator, offering comparable advantages to the ancestors of modern prairie birds. The fossil record is not complete enough for us to reconstruct the world south of the Great Ice during its maximum expansions in Pleistocene times.

For birds the wealth of the grasslands lies in plants that are green for a short growing season, in the grains that they produce in abundance, and in the dead, dry tops of plants that go dormant during the summer drought. Few birds are equipped to rely upon prairie foliage for more than nesting material and a modicum of concealment. They benefit instead from the grain, which is so rich in nourishment and from insects that feed on the plants. Generally avoiding the small rodents of the plains, which compete with birds for food and shelter, they raise their families and then depart. Or, as birds of prey, they patrol vast areas of open country, seeking meals of suitable size in the form of animals that have lost their saving wariness through accident, overcrowding, or disease. Whether the victim is a grasshopper, a mouse, or even a small bird makes little difference; all of their prey prove to be surplus animals, for which even the wide world of the open prairie offers insufficient space.

Like ancient Gaul, the bird life of the grasslands seems naturally divided into thirds. One group is of seed-eaters, which may space out their meals or feed their young with whatever insects they can catch. Another third are the birds of prey, few of them present in any numbers or with real regularity. The remainder include opportunists of a different sort: scavengers, cranes, and shorebirds which may stay a while during migration, taking on fuel for further flight.

Of the seed-eaters, only the sharp-tailed grouse and the two kinds of prairie chickens are large enough to be regarded as game birds. This, and their nonmigratory habits, may be their undoing. Prairie chickens in particular have been dwindling away during the past two centuries, unable to find enough food and cover on prairies that are plowed under and planted with cultivated crops. Now they are on the danger list, and their eastern counterpart—the heath hen— is already extinct.

The smaller seed-eaters find food and cover among the crops, are totally respected as song birds (largely because of the number of pest insects they eat) and travel south for the winter. The largest of them, the **lark bunting,** is distinctive and popular enough to have been chosen the state bird of Colorado. Only the male is eye-catching. He acts like a bobolink, singing on the wing, the large white areas on his wings contrasting with the blue-black of the remainder of his body. In flight he spreads the feathers of his tail slightly, showing white narrowly along each side and some more at the square tip. His song is far more varied than a bobolink's, and he lacks the yellow nape and white rump of this bird, so similar in size and shape, which belongs to an entirely different family.

Lark Bunting
Calamospiza melanocorys
Length 5½" to 7½"

Chestnut-Collared Longspur
Calcarius ornatus
Length 5½″ to 6½″

McCown's Longspur
Rhynchophanes mccownii
Length 5¾″ to 6″

Dickcissel
Spiza americana
Length 6″ to 7″

The female lark bunting and the male in his winter plumage seem just plain sparrows with a white edge on the tail. They differ only in details from similarly marked sparrows that flit about in the same prairies, picking up seeds and occasional insects from the ground. The vesper sparrows have forked tails with a wider white edging, and the young of lark sparrows rounded tails that are tipped as well as edged in white. Even the savannah sparrows, with plain, dark, forked tails, are marked much the same. These color patterns have survival value, for they blend magnificently with the ground when seen from the altitude of a cruising hawk. The birds themselves pick out little clues in markings, antics, and sounds that let them recognize members of their own kind in a mixed flock.

Sometimes a savannah sparrow runs, but rarely does one walk; usually it either hops or takes to its wings. Walking and running birds of sparrow size upon the grasslands are usually the gregarious longspurs, which warble pleasantly as they fly in flocks. They are named for the extended claws on their long hind toes, which may be just a little longer and extended than those on other kinds of sparrows. The more prevalent is the **chestnut-collared longspur,** the male of which wears a reddish-brown band across the back of his neck where the less common **McCown's longspur** is gray. He also has a much greater expanse of black on his chest and shows differences in the markings on the sides of his head and on his tail. The females of these longspurs appear to be just sparrows with brown streaks on back and sides. The female McCown's has a T-shaped dark mark on the top of her tail, as does the male. In the chestnut-collared, this dark area is an isosceles triangle with the point toward the body.

From the Canadian border to central Texas and from the Appalachians to the foothills of the Rockies, loose colonies of nesting **dickcissels** add to the number of sparrow-like birds on the Great Plains. Except for her all-dark tail, the female resembles a vesper sparrow or a McCown's longspur. Her mate wears the distinctive black bib with lemon-yellow below it, and is more likely to find a conspicuous perch on which to sing *DICK, DICK-cissel.* Sometimes his voice sounds astonishingly like that of another prairie bird—the western meadowlark—which is larger and has a big black V across its golden-yellow chest. Dickcissels on migration often visit the east

North American Birds

coast and Florida. Almost all spend the cold months in the Tropics, from southern Mexico into South America. A few become exceptions, staying all winter and joining sparrows at the feeding trays that people set out when snow and bad weather block access to wild foods.

To the prairie provinces of Canada, **horned larks** come each summer from farther south. Members of the prairie race of this modest little bird, they have yellow only on the throat. Both sexes are marked in much the same way: a black mark across the chest, another downcurved through each eye, a black tail edged in white, and two black feathers like backward-slanting horns pointing from the brows. Despite these features, which seem so distinctive when a horned lark is seen against a plain background, the bird can vanish in its native grasslands merely by crouching and remaining absolutely still. It also runs along the ground almost like a mouse, and its markings help break up its outline. Even the little horns fold back and disappear.

Horned Lark
Eremophila alpestris
Length 7″ to 8″

Over The Grasslands

Seed-eating birds all show this same flat-to-the-ground response when they discern a hawk of any kind approaching. Besides this inherited reaction, they gain another protective advantage from their environment; an uninterrupted view of the sky in all directions at once. Ordinarily they see a predator flapping over the grasslands or soaring along several seconds before they themselves can be seen from above.

They are in greatest danger when the arriving predator is a **prairie falcon.** Alternately flapping and gliding, it flies rapidly and low, pausing occasionally to hover and drop on whatever victim its sharp eyes have detected. Whenever birds and mammals are scarce or too well camouflaged, it takes grasshoppers and crickets. Fortunately for grassland creatures, the prairie falcons spread their hunting over a wide range, including wooded territory to the Pacific Coast and western Canada, and south in winter to northern Mexico. For a nest site, these falcons hunt out an inaccessible ledge and radiate out from there to find food for their young.

Prairie Falcon
Falco mexicanus
Length 17″ to 20″; Wingspread 40″ to 42″

North American Birds

The smallest and most common falcon in open country is the **sparrow hawk.** Occasionally it merits the name it has been given by capturing a small sparrow, but with a body only the size of a robin's, the sparrow hawk is hardly big enough to tackle larger prey. Most of its food, in fact, consists of insects and mice, although it takes also spiders, small lizards, and sometimes an amphibian. This little hawk cannot pause long enough on its migrations to seriously harass the birds of grasslands. In the Great Plains it is merely on its way, to or from its winter territory in Mexico and the Gulf States. Its nest sites are in hollow trees and old woodpecker holes along the fringe of woodland between New England and Alaska.

Sparrow Hawk
Falco sparverius
Length 9" to 12"

Over The Grasslands

Most of the large hawks, likewise, are en route elsewhere when they fly over grasslands. They need tall forest trees as places to nest, and these are generally far away. The largest of these visitors is likely to be the **ferruginous hawk,** a specialist that feeds exclusively on rodents. It is strictly a western hunter, ranging north into the Canadian prairies and southward for the winter into Mexico. But the small birds take no chances when a ferruginous appears. They crouch silently until the hawk moves on, soaring off on wings with a 54-inch span.

Ferruginous Hawk
Buteo regalis
Length 22½″ to 25″; Wingspread 56″

Swainson's hawk is a more frequent menace. It glides, holding its 49-inch wings in a wide dihedral, covering the territory west of the Mississippi into Canada and all the way to Alaska. Like the widespread red-tailed hawk of similar size, heavier body and slower action, and like the more slender, smaller red-shouldered hawk that ranges into the prairie states from the American Southeast, the Swainson's has the habit of settling on a perch close to the ground and simply waiting there, motionless. Eventually some small rodent, bird, or an insect is likely to reveal its whereabouts and become a meal.

The marsh hawk and the short-eared owl, both among the most widespread of North American birds, pose a serious problem to seed-eaters of the grasslands because they nest on the ground and can make themselves at home almost anywhere. The marsh hawk glides over the prairies, its wings upraised, tilting from side to side as though to pounce. It hunts only a few feet above the ground, and frequently beats its 20-inch wings to hover in one place before dropping to the kill. Mostly it catches rodents, but small birds are second choice, and insects a poor third.

The **short-eared owl** does not wait for nightfall to go hunting. It often flies in search of food on dull days and while the sun is low.

Swainson's Hawk
Buteo swainsoni
Length 19″ to 22″; Wingspread 49″

Short-Eared Owl
Asio flammeus
Length 13″ to 17″

North American Birds

With wings raised in a dihedral like that of the marsh hawk, it glides along, capturing many a small bird as well as its favorite mice, moles, and grasshoppers.

The little short-tailed **burrowing owls,** which feed almost exclusively on insects, rarely fly farther than to the nearest fence post as a perch. On the Florida prairies near Lake Okeechobee they dig their own nest burrows, but on the Great Plains they have developed a considerable dependence upon the once-widespread prairie dogs, nesting inside abandoned tunnels. Burrowing owls are active by day rather than at night, and often bob up and down on their long legs as though trying to get a better measure of distance to objects that may be edible or dangerous. Paralleling the decline in numbers of prairie dogs, and of grasshoppers on croplands (both mostly due to

Burrowing Owl
Speotyto cunicularia
Length 9"

chemical control measures), the number of burrowing owls on the western prairies has greatly decreased. Those that are seen are frequently residents of the mowed grassy areas beside airport runways, where no one comes with plow or spray truck. Despite the noise and commotion of aircraft taking off and landing, airports can become little islands of prairie bird life amid immense areas of cultivated land.

The Great Plains and other grasslands in North America include a good many low places which trap enough moisture to maintain a few cottonwood trees and perhaps some marsh vegetation. These prairie oases are too valuable to fill in and, while they exist, provide opportunities for birds we ordinarily associate with the edges of open water. The **sandhill cranes** walk about sedately, or fly with neck outstretched and long legs trailing, stopping now and again to stab at a frog, small reptile, big insects, or mouse; or to pick neatly at some grain or edible plants growing in shallow water. The migratory western race was once far more widespread than at present; now these birds return from wintering grounds in Mexico and southern California to the Canadian prairie provinces and British Columbia, north to the Arctic and south into a few northwestern and central states. A nonmigratory race is at home in the prairies of Florida and Cuba. Still another race occupies similar territory in Siberia.

Sandhill Crane
Grus canadensis
Length 40″ to 48″; Wingspread 80″

North American Birds

Compared to the sandhill crane, which stands four feet tall and boasts a wing spread of seven feet, all other birds of the broad grasslands seem small. Even the **golden eagle,** now growing rare, has a smaller body, shorter legs, and wings not more than six and a half feet tip to tip. In migration, these eagles pass over the Great Plains, stopping occasionally to feed. Generally they catch rodents, but almost any small bird is acceptable; so is carrion, for eagles are close kin to the scavenging vultures.

Golden Eagle
Aquila chrysaetos
Length 30″ to 41″; Wingspread 79″ to 87″

Over The Grasslands

South of the Canadian border, the turkey vulture is the principal scavenger of the grasslands. Along the Mexican border of Arizona and New Mexico, it is often joined at a carcass by the long-legged **Audubon's caracara,** whose likeness decorates Mexico's official coat of arms. The caracara is common in Mexico and southward to northern South America, feasting on carrion or pouncing on snakes, lizards, turtles, and small rodents. This bird follows the same habits in southern Florida, where it is nonmigratory and spends most of its time on the ground.

Audubon's Caracara
Caracara cheriway
Length 22″; Wingspread 48″

North American Birds

Generally we think of gulls as scavengers. But the gull of the prairies is **Franklin's gull,** an insect-eater with a black head and a patch of white followed by black at the tip of its gray wings. If frogs, mollusks, or small fish are available in shallow water, Franklin's gull will eat them too. Often it finds a wet place on the plains and feeds among shorebirds, particularly the little killdeers with their black-banded chests, common over most of North America, and some western birds that roam less widely: the mountain plover, the upland plover, the marbled godwit, and Wilson's phalarope. Without being

Franklin's Gull
Larus pipixcan
Length 13½″ to 15½″

Over The Grasslands

told, we could easily conclude that the **mountain plover** was just a killdeer that had not yet developed its black neck bands and the black stripe from beak to nape below the eye. But the mountain plover has long and varied whistles, never the *DEE, kill-DEE,* for which the killdeer is named. And it breeds on the flatlands along the east side of the Rocky Mountains, flying afterwards to Mexico, while the killdeers range from farther east and west to farther north, and often spend the winter in the southern United States.

Mountain Plover
Eupoda montana
Length 8″ to 9½″

North American Birds

The **upland plover** is actually a big sandpiper of the grasslands, with a mellow whistle, a long neck, long legs, and fairly long tail. In traveling from its nesting grounds, which range from Alaska to the north-central United States and New England, it overflies most of North America east of the Rockies to spend the winter in southern South America. The **marbled godwit** is a sandpiper too, but is a big bird—as much as 20 inches long—with a four-and-a-half-inch beak that may be slightly upcurved. It calls *god-WIT*, *god-WIT*, and then flies off crying repeatedly *queep!*

Upland Plover
Bartramia longicauda
Length 11″ to 12½″

Marbled Godwit
Limosa fedoa
Length 16″ to 20″

North American Birds

Wilson's phalarope looks and acts like a sandpiper in flight and on the ground except, perhaps, that its beak, neck, and legs are a trifle long. But in the water these birds swim and spin around expertly, propelling themselves with toes that are lobed and serve as fins. They stir up the bottom and then reach for the insects that try to return to a hiding place. This is one of the strange species in which the female is larger and more colorful in summer than the male. She puts on the display, lays the eggs, and then provides the distraction while he incubates and broods. Wilson's phalarope is the landlubber of this family of shorebirds, and finds homes in the northwestern United States and adjacent Canada all the way up through the prairie provinces.

Wilson's Phalarope
Steganopus tricolor
Length 8½″ to 10″

Over The Grasslands

The total area in the grasslands where a phalarope can go swimming is mighty small. Essentially these plains are a two-dimensional world, with every kind of life on about the same level. Drought comes regularly by midsummer and puts an end to the productivity of the plants. They can utilize only about a third as much energy from the sun each year as the trees can on an equal area of deciduous forest. Drought, rare in forested country, makes the difference. On the grasslands, with a third as much solar energy being transformed into foodstuffs, there are about a third as many kinds of birds as find homes among the trees.

Costa's Hummingbird
Calypte costae
Length 3″ to 3½″

CHAPTER FIVE

DESERTS AND DRY COUNTRY

BEFORE SO MANY PEOPLE MOVED TO THE SOUTHWESTERN STATES AND PAID TO have water brought from deep wells or diversions of the Colorado River, we used to hear about the "Great American Desert." It is still a part of the country where, for most of the summer growing season, the combined effects of hot sun and dry winds could easily evaporate at least twice as much moisture as actually falls. The native kinds of vegetation and the plant invaders from foreign lands are all specialists in surviving chronic drought. The animals that live there are equally well adapted to get moisture and food from the plants, either directly or indirectly. A hummingbird gets food and water directly by sucking nectar from cactus flowers and a warbler indirectly, by eating insects that feed on cactus.

In late winter and early spring, when rains are more frequent and the desert plants open more flowers, hummingbirds of more than half a dozen kinds fly north into southern Texas, New Mexico, Arizona, and California. But only **Costa's hummer,** the size of the ruby-throated east of the Mississippi, stays in the deserts most of the year and finds what it needs to live. The male has an iridescent purple head and, growing from the sides of his throat, long feathers that

157

he can extend like a bib over his white chest. His mate and fully-feathered young are mostly green and, like him, have somewhat blacker plumes in the sides of their fan-shaped tails. A family of hummers is ordinarily on its own by the time the shrubby sage-brush opens its heads of inconspicuous yellow flowers. But neither adult nor young have difficulty lowering themselves helicopter fashion between the stiff branches and silver-gray leaves to reach the nectar.

Between these shrubs, **sage grouse** run freely without disturbing the hummingbirds. The parent grouse, which may weigh eight pounds each, are the biggest of American grouse and the largest birds that subsist on plant materials in dry country. On foot they travel into the hills for the summer, and back down to the plains before winter sets in. In spring, the males find special mating grounds on the plains and put on their amazing displays. Each male faces another in the group, fans out his tail into a radiating pattern of pointed feathers, and puffs out his chest until his black collar disappears and the white feathers scarcely cover the distended skin. Suddenly he inflates a pair of air sacs at the front of his short neck. Like two bright oranges, they push out between the white feathers and throb in time with the deep booming calls he utters in quick succession. They are resonators as well as marks of his maleness and health, and help extend his vocal invitation for female sage grouse to approach when ready.

Sage Grouse
Centrocercus urophasianus
Length 22" to 30"

Deserts And Dry Country

Birds of similar form—though much smaller, usually weighing less than six ounces each—are the desert quails of dry lands somewhat farther south. Both sexes of the **scaled quail** are alike in plumage, the bluish feathers of throat and back rimmed in dark brown which gives the appearance of overlapping scales. The male raises the feathers of his crown into a crest that is cottony white, and calls in a sharp whistle *be-CAUSE, be-CAUSE!* Yet where the range of scaled quails overlaps with that of Gambel's quail, mixed flocks are often seen and some cross-breeding takes place. Both sexes of Gambel's wear a prominent recurved topknot, and have no brown edging on the feathers of the chest. The male Gambel's has a black face and head, a black spot on his white underside, and produces a quite different three-syllabled call. These handsome little birds and their chicks stay together for many months, feeding largely on insects in summer and plant material when the weather becomes colder. Probably, back before the Ice Ages, the Gambel's quails and scaled quails had ancestors in common.

Scaled Quail
Callipepla squamata
Length 10″ to 12″

North American Birds

Mesquite trees provide food and shelter for even more kinds of desert life, partly because their roots grow quickly to great depth and are able to reach underground water during some of the longest droughts. The quail often hide among the thorn-studded lower branches which droop to the ground. Brown-gray crested **pyrrhuloxias** build their cup-shaped nests where mesquite branches will provide support and protection. When the seed pods ripen on the tree, the pyrrhuloxias pick them off and crack them open. But when caterpillars or grasshoppers or weevils are available, these relatives of the cardinal prefer the insects to any seeds. These birds are non-migratory residents of mesquite country in the Southwest from southeast Texas to southern Arizona and down to central Mexico.

Pyrrhuloxia
Pyrrhuloxia sinuata
Length 7½″ to 8¼″

Deserts And Dry Country

In some of these areas and in California near the Mexican border, a mesquite tree along a dry wash through the desert is likely to provide a nesting place for a pair of **white-winged doves.** These seed-eaters are common farther south, but often spread a short distance north of the border into the United States. In 1961 they were discovered to be important pollinators of flowers on the giant saguaro cacti, performing the task inadvertently when they visit this state flower of Arizona for nectar in the early morning. White-winged doves are slightly smaller than a domestic pigeon, and show white areas on their wings and on the back corners of their rounded tails while perching or walking along the ground. The white on the wings becomes more conspicuous when the birds fly since, beyond the bend of the wing, the feathers are all a contrasting black.

White-Winged Dove
Zenaida asiatica
Length 11″ to 12½″

Inca Dove
Scardafella inca
Length 7½″ to 8″

Black-Throated Sparrow
Amphispiza bilineata
Length 4¾″ to 5¼″

Sage Sparrow
Amphispiza belli
Length 5″ to 6″

The little **Inca doves,** which match the white-wingeds in geograph-ical range and food preferences, are only about half the size. An Inca has white corners on its long tail, but no white on its wings. Often this bird is called a "scaled dove" because the blue-gray feathers on its back, rump, and the area of wing exposed while the dove is walk-ing are edged in dark brown, producing a scale-like pattern.

The sparrows of desert country are only slightly smaller than Inca doves. The more widespread is the **black-throated sparrow,** which often perches on a twig of sagebrush to sing its sweet, high-pitched trill. It nests on the ground, choosing sites from northern Nevada and southwestern Colorado well down into Mexico, retiring even farther south when winter comes. Over a part of this range the black-throats compete for seeds and insects with the **sage sparrow,** which has a dark spot in the middle of its white breast and a habit of flick-ing its white-edged tail.

Almost the only other birds of dry country that benefit from the plants directly are the desert horned larks, the crested phainopeplas, and the pinyon jays. A **phainopepla** is actually a silky flycatcher and does pursue insects on the wing, flying after them from a prominent perch if such can be found. At these times, the white patch on the outer wing feathers of the male shows conspicuously in contrast with the dark blue of his other plumage; his mate and young are brownish gray. At other times, the phainopeplas peck at flower heads that have gone to seed, or pick small fruits from the ground, uttering an occa-sional high-pitched short whistle. They are much more solitary than waxwings, which they resemble in size and silhouette. Pinyon jays are much more sociable birds. Frequently they wander from the scrubby forests of pinyon pine where they nest to seek seeds and insects under the sagebrush and among the low cactus plants. The adults are dull blue, the juveniles a lavender-gray. While perched they often call continuously *QUEH-QUEH-QUEH*, but in flight the note changes to a mew.

Phainopepla
Phainopepla nitens
Length 7" to 7¾"

North American Birds

Insects are the prime targets for many of the desert birds. Although small, prey of this kind provides both nourishment and much needed moisture. Generally the birds that rely upon insects for food need not expend their energy to search out open water from which to drink. So long as they find enough to eat, their thirst remains satisfied. This may explain why Say's phoebe thrives in the dry lands as well as on ranches all the way from interior Alaska to Mexico. It is slightly larger than the eastern phoebe and acts in the same way, even to wagging its tail downward at intervals and calling plaintively *PHU-WEER.*

The American Southwest is home to the spectacular **scissor-tailed flycatcher,** the state bird of Oklahoma, which builds a nest of sticks on low limbs of deciduous trees such as the widespread mesquites. Whenever perched, watching for an insect to chase, the birds lets its extraordinarily long tail droop downward. But in flight, it spreads and closes the feathers in two groups as though they were the blades of a pair of scissors. Some of these antics may be necessary to control the irregular flight needed in following a dodging insect, but the rest is sheerly for display. The female and young have somewhat shorter tails but behave in the same manner. For the winter, most scissor-tailed flycatchers migrate to northern Mexico, but a few follow the Gulf of Mexico to hunt insects over the dry prairies of southern Florida.

Scissor-Tailed Flycatcher
Muscivora forficata
Length 11½" to 15"

Deserts And Dry Country

Vermilion flycatchers are primarily birds of Mexico and tropical America. In summer they come across the border into adjacent states from southeastern California to southern Texas. Perched on a telephone wire, watching for an insect to fly by, the male vermilion is a flaming spot against the summer sky. His beak is black, and a dark streak crosses from beak to nape, matching the dark brown of back and wings and tail. His mate is mostly brownish-gray above, with a white throat and dark streaks down the chest onto a salmon-pink

Vermilion Flycatcher
Pyrocephalus rubinus
Length 5½″ to 6½″

North American Birds

area which extends to the dark tail. The streaks and the pink coloration distinguish her easily from Say's phoebe, as does her smaller size. Vermilion flycatchers often sing in flight, sometimes hovering while uttering their high-pitched sputtering melody. In both ways they differ markedly from the **white-throated swifts** which sometimes pursue insects higher and faster and more erratically over the same deserts. The swifts have longer, pointed wings and a smaller head with a shorter beak. Against the sky it is often hard to see the white sides, the white line above the eye, and the long white pointed bib that extends almost to the base of the notched tail. White-throateds are strictly western birds, traveling in summer as far north as British Columbia; in winter they find what they need to eat in southern California and into Central America.

White-Throated Swift
Aeronautes saxatalis
Length 6" to 7"

Deserts And Dry Country

Desert country produces enough small insects to attract quite a variety of small birds that inspect the surfaces of plants for food. Some of the long-tailed relatives of chickadees are even smaller and more agile than the wrens. Both the **yellow-headed verdin** and the **common bushtit** are noticeably smaller than a house wren, and both flip and chatter through the sagebrush and other scrub of dry areas in the Southwest. Mature verdins have a spot of rusty red on the shoulder. The juveniles lack it and are often hard to tell from bushtits, especially when both kinds flock together and seem constantly in motion.

Verdin
Auriparus flaviceps
Length 4″ to 4½″

Common Bushtit
Psaltriparus minimus
Length 3¾″ to 4¼″

Wrentit
Chamaea fasciata
Length 6″ to 6½″

Cactus Wren
Campylorhynchus brunneicapillum
Length 7″ to 8¾″

Deserts And Dry Country

In dense chaparral, the secretive and considerably larger **wrentits** hunt close to the Pacific coast and part way down into Baja California. Their loud songs, which begin with a few staccato chirps and continue with a trill all in the same key, become tantalizing since the singer remains hidden. The bird itself is a nondescript brown with streaky breast and white eyes. It keeps its long tail uptilted most of the time, apparently balancing for the next hop through the undergrowth.

The **cactus wren**—the state bird of Arizona—is as big as some thrushes, and wears a similar pattern of dark spots on throat and breast with smaller dots underneath. Its song, too, is a monotone in low key. Its magic, however, lies in its ability to carry nesting material into a fork of some dangerously spiny cactus (such as a jumping cholla) and build a nursery without getting impaled. We have watched one, its beak full of insects for its nestlings, flipping from one cactus branch to another, standing on and among spines and stiff bristles that would have penetrated our skin at a touch, warily waiting for us to depart before going to the nest we had discovered.

Neither the cactus wren nor the **canyon wren** finds a need to migrate from their home territories in northern Mexico and the adjacent United States. The canyon wren shows a preference for steep rocky hillsides and canyon walls and gains more shelter and perhaps more food than the cactus wren can find on open deserts. Seemingly in consequence, canyon wrens range northward in dry country into British Columbia. Their whistled songs descend in pitch, and draw attention to the brown singer whose snow-white throat and breast contrast with a chestnut-colored underside.

Canyon Wren
Catherpes mexicanus
Length 4½″ to 5¾″

Lucy's Warbler
Vermivora luciae
Length 4″

California Thrasher
Toxostoma redivivum
Length 11″ to 13″

On stony and rocky ground, even seemingly barren highlands, the rock wrens walk along, bobbing their bodies as they go and singing a great variety of trilling songs. These little birds, also distinctive for having a pale breast streaked narrowly with brown, hunt out secluded places among rocks or on ledges for their cup-shaped nests, built of grasses and whatever bits of moss they can find. Generally they carry little stones to the vicinity of the nest, as though to pave the approach the wrens customarily take. For the winter, the rock wrens retire to suitable country in Mexico or just north of the border. But each summer they migrate early, some to homes in rocky barrens in southern British Columbia and eastward almost to the Mississippi River.

Far more stereotyped in phrasing are the songs of **Lucy's warbler,** a small, gray-backed bird with white underparts that winters in western Mexico and nests where it can find small holes in trees on deserts of the southwestern United States. Often it discovers a suitable cavity where a storm has torn a branch from a mesquite tree. Judging from the small size of the insects a pair of Lucy's warblers bring back for their young, these birds must benefit the vegetation on all sides of their nest site, often catching a newly hatched caterpillar before it has had time to do much damage.

As the size of the bird increases, so does the average size of the insects it eats. Often we can make a good estimate of the growth of nestlings in a nest we haven't found, just from the dimensions of the caterpillars the parent birds are carrying back to their home territory. New-hatched young need tiny flies. Fledglings that are almost ready to leave the nest seem able to swallow insects that would strain a parent's beak.

When house finches fly into the deserts in search of food, as they often do, they ordinarily look for something larger than what a warbler or a bushtit needs. The finches' bills are equipped to crack open the hard coverings on many seeds that have no appeal whatever to birds that prefer insects.

Birds generally choose definite levels at which to forage, even when they seem ready to accept a wide variety of fruits and insects. The big **California thrasher,** which is an unstreaked bird with dark eyes, uses its long curved beak to dig into the earth for the tidbits it eats. It runs along the ground with its head low and its long tail

North American Birds

almost vertical, flying much less than other thrashers. Perhaps these habits limit its distribution, for it is found only close to the Pacific coast from northern Baja California to a short distance beyond San Francisco. By contrast, the little **sage thrasher** ranges north into British Columbia and southeast to the panhandle of Texas. This bird has a short beak, yellow eyes, a streaked breast, and white corners to the dark brown tail which it holds high while running along the ground or while pausing to scratch with both feet at once. Displacing sticks, stones, and fallen leaves, the thrasher exposes a wonderful assortment of hidden seeds, fruits and insects.

Sage Thrasher
Oreoscoptes montanus
Length 8″ to 9″

Deserts And Dry Country

Perhaps the assortment of food that appeals to a sage thrasher differs from that chosen by a **green-tailed towhee,** for these towhees act in an almost identical way under the same sagebrush, have a similar nesting range, and retire for the winter to a corresponding area—from Baja California and northern Mexico into the adjacent deserts from California to Texas. Both sexes of the towhee have the white throat and belly, the green wings and tail. But only the male wears the rusty crown and gray along the sides of the body.

At a higher level in the desert, **Scott's oriole** explores the taller vegetation, nesting also in a pinyon pine, high juniper, or Joshua

Green-Tailed Towhee
Chlorura chlorura
Length 6¼" to 7"

Scott's Oriole
Icterus parisorum
Length 7¼" to 8¼"

North American Birds

tree. Seeing the bird clinging to a flower stalk of a yucca or a century plant, you'll have a chance to assure yourself that, though sounding like a western meadowlark, the songster is actually an oriole. The male will be bright lemon-yellow except for the black on his head, chest, back, wings, and the central portion and tip of his tail. The female and young are a duller greenish-yellow, with a dark tail and wings but no real black anywhere; the dark streaks on their yellow backs are distinctive. Like other orioles, they seek a mixed diet of insects and fruit and weave a pendant sac-like nest below a tree branch.

A different food supply is available to birds that drill into trees and large cacti to reach the insects boring inside. The southwestern deserts have two woodpeckers that get the bulk of their food that way, but that turn also to cactus fruits for nourishment. The smaller, known both as the **ladder-backed** and the **cactus woodpecker,** has the larger range, nesting northward beyond Mexico as far as Utah and southwestern Kansas. The male has a red cap, the female a black one; both wear black streaks on the cheeks and finer ones on breast and sides. The larger **Gila woodpecker,** which is known also as the gray-breasted woodpecker and the desert woodpecker, excavates its nest burrows in saguaros and other giant cacti in western Mexico, Baja California, and low arid areas from southeastern California to southwestern New Mexico. These males too have a red cap (the females have none). The Gila resembles the ladder-backed in having a black back crossed by a succession of white markings. The Gila, however, has no black on its face or chest or sides, all being a sandy brown.

Ladder-Backed Woodpecker
Dendrocopos scalaris
Length 6″ to 7½″

Gila Woodpecker
Centurus uropygialis
Length 8″ to 10″

North American Birds

Abandoned nest holes of Gila woodpeckers seldom go to waste. They are often used by the **elf owl** as a nest site or a resting place for the day. Although the elf is expert at catching insects in the air, its specialty is in disarming scorpions. Smartly, the little owl nips off the scorpion's stinger-tipped tail. To do so in darkness without getting stung must be exciting work. While feeding in this way, the bird chatters an almost continuous call. To find its food reliably all year long, it migrates between winter quarters in central Mexico and the deserts from southeastern California to southwestern Texas.

Only one of the small feathered denizens of dry country seems really out of place there. It is the mountain plover, so obviously a shore bird that a person automatically looks for water when a small flock runs along the desert floor or flies low over it, wings drooping, ready for instant landing. But this widespread prairie bird seeks insects even on the most arid ground and among sagebrush thickets where open water is a mirage. It may even nest under a desert shrub, as if to prove its adaptability.

The **roadrunner** seems almost reluctant to take to its wings. Few birds are more typical of the arid Southwest—yet this one is actually a giant cuckoo with a long white-tipped tail and a shaggy crest. It is often seen catching lizards and snakes, then swallowing its prey a little at a time. Less obvious are the countless insects and spiders (and even mice) that it takes at a single gulp. The roadrunner constructs a coarse cup-shaped nest of twigs in a mesquite tree or tall cactus, but sings its dove-like notes while standing on the ground.

Elf Owl
Micrathene whitneyi
Length 5" to 6"

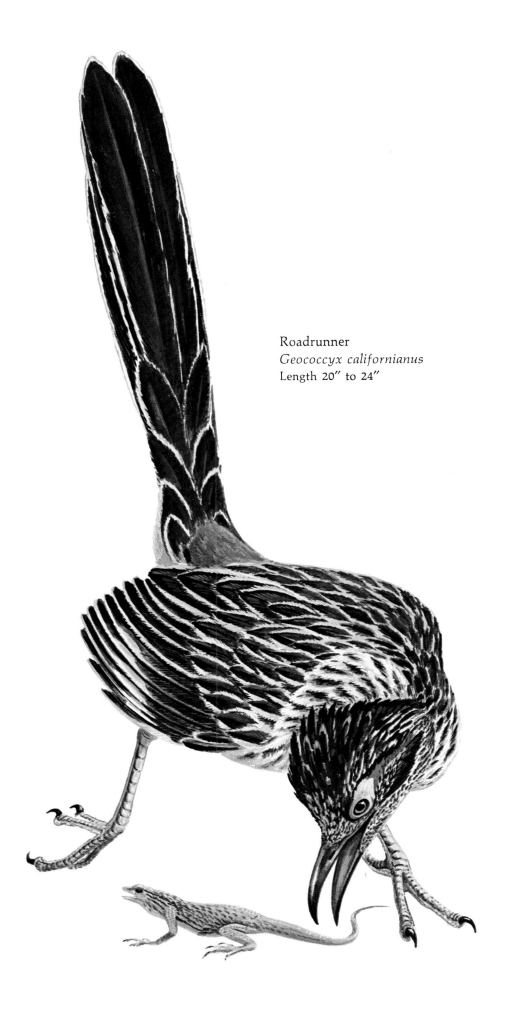

Roadrunner
Geococcyx californianus
Length 20″ to 24″

North American Birds

Larger birds of prey appear more sporadically over each area of the dry Southwest. The golden eagle, now growing rare everywhere on the continent, flies through the most remote desert in hunting for rodents. Both the red-tailed hawk and the ferruginous hawk wander from grasslands into desert upon occasion, as though checking to see whether a regular route might be worth the effort. The big **Harris' hawk,** with bright chestnut-colored feathers on shoulders and upper legs, soars north out of Mexico and patrols the brushlands beyond the border. It seldom invades real desert while seeking mice, reptiles, and an occasional small bird. Nor does Audubon's caracara go far into Texas, New Mexico, or Arizona from its homelands in Mexico and Central America. It cannot soar as efficiently as the black vulture or the turkey vulture, and consequently must work harder for the carrion and the prey it finds.

Harris' Hawk
Parabuteo unicinctus
Length 17½″ to 29″; Wingspread 42″ to 45″

Deserts And Dry Country

The most magnificent of all soaring birds in North America, the **California condor,** must once have been widespread over the dry hills and valleys now densely clad in sagebrush. Now this great bird with its wing span to 10½ feet is on the danger list, limited to a small mountainous area of southern California near the coast. To some extent, its decline is due to man's success in controlling brush fires, which otherwise would bare the land and keep the sagebrush low enough for condors to see sick animals and carcasses upon the ground.

Dry country always presents a harsh challenge to life of any kind. To make a home in it requires extraordinary adaptations in body and behavior, and it is significant that so many birds have met the challenge with apparent grace.

California Condor
Gymnogyps californianus
Length 45″ to 55″; Wingspread 102″ to 114″

CHAPTER SIX

BEYOND THE TIMBERLINE

NORTH AMERICAN BIRDS ANSWER THE QUESTION: "HOW HIGH MUST A mountain be to offer special opportunities?" through their inherited choice of places to nest. High slopes are sought out regularly by feathered migrants that will raise their families nowhere else. But no peak or mountain chain east of the Rockies provides amenities a bird can't find more easily by going north. Only in the West do there seem to be special opportunities afforded by higher elevation.

The average hiker may feel that traversing slopes and precipices requires a great deal of energy. But for a bird on the wing, the cost of upward flight is trivial compared to the routine exertions of finding food, escaping pursuit, and protecting a mate and young. On mountains, the benefits are largely climatic features and what plants rainfall and temperature may permit. Days are longer on a mountain, for the sun's rays strike the peak earlier at dawn, and linger longer at sunset. For a bird that spends most of the daylit hours foraging by eye, the extra daylight has immense importance.

Sometimes it seems that each level on the mountain from the foothills to the peak has its own bird population. To climb and visit them in succession is almost like riding the escalator past various

181

floors in a big department store. Each kind of mountain bird has its own "department" or level on high country all the way from the Mexican boundary into Alaska.

Perhaps man's general impatience in climbing explains why the "mountain" quail, the "mountain" bluebird and the "mountain" chickadee are all found in the foothills. The **mountain quail** is the largest of North American quails, a bird that runs adroitly through the underbrush in mixed woodlands and chaparral. Both sexes are handsomely marked with vertical white stripes on the flanks and wear a tall slim head plume that waves around as the birds run and peck at food on the ground. During the breeding season, males utter isolated mellow calls suggesting the *caw* of a crow. When alarmed, mountain quails of both sexes communicate with frequent high-pitched whistled notes. They are heard through a considerable range of territory, in mountains from Baja California to Washington and Idaho. The birds wander widely but can scarcely be said to migrate.

Mountain Quail
Oreortyx pictus
Length 10½" to 11½"

Beyond The Timberline

The mountain bluebird needs open spaces where it can find insects and small fruits upon the ground. This restricts it to the full sunlight of more open woodlands and forest borders where it can see, can hover and pounce on its prey without danger from hidden predators. It builds its nest in a hollow stump or a low tree hole, mostly of grasses gathered in the open.

Mountain chickadees flip acrobatically among the tree branches, inspecting the smallest twigs for insects and their eggs. The bird is distinctive for having a white line above the black stripe through its eye. Seemingly it has little need to migrate, and it is a resident in mountain woodlands from Baja California to far north in British Columbia, and eastward to those of New Mexico.

In southwestern New Mexico, southeast and central Arizona and Mexico south to Oaxaca, mountain chickadees often flock with **bridled titmice** of about the same size. This titmouse has a peaked crest, a white face, and a V-shaped black marking through the eye. The

Mountain Chickadee
Parus gambeli
Length 5″ to 5¾″

Bridled Titmouse
Parus wollweberi
Length 4½″ to 5″

North American Birds

V points backward toward the neck, the lower arm of it extending forward to join with a black chin spot. Since titmice and chickadees hunt for similar food and nest in comparable tree holes, the two species must compete with one another more than their sociable antics would suggest.

Despite the bitter tannins in oak leaves and the resin in pine needles, both oaks and pines attract many kinds of small insects. Sharp-eyed little birds find the mixed woodlands a happy hunting ground. Such high country in southern Arizona attracts the **painted redstarts,** widespread in similar places southward through Mexico in Central America. Both sexes are mostly black, with a blood-red patch on the lower breast and white from there to below the tail. Their tails are white on the sides, and their wings bear white patches. Warbling softly, painted redstarts hover and dart among the foliage, picking off bugs, flies, and caterpillars in the liveliest way.

Painted Redstart
Septopnaga ruticilla
Length 4½″ to 5½″

Beyond The Timberline

The larger **coppery-tailed trogons** come to these same mountain woodlands, but sit about on exposed branches of the trees for much of the day, letting their long tails droop downward almost vertically. Only the male has copper-colored tail feathers, each black at the tip. His back glints with a metallic green luster that sometimes appears to be a golden-bronze. His mate has a white ear-patch and only disconnected areas of pink on her undersides, where the male is a bright rosy red. Like her back and wings, her tail is grayish-brown above but marked below with three pairs of large white spots, between which it is streaked crosswise with black. These handsome birds are fruit-eaters native to much of Mexico, but in Arizona and extreme southern Texas they find the food and the nest cavities in trees that they require.

Coppery-Tailed Trogon
Trogon elegans
Length 11″ to 12″

Acorn Woodpecker
Melanerpes formicivorus
Length 8″ to 9½″

Broad-Tailed Hummingbird
Selasphorus platycercus
Length 4″ to 4½″

Black-Chinned Hummingbird
Archilochus alexandri
Length 3⅓″ to 3¾″

Beyond The Timberline

Some of the holes they seek are the work of the **acorn woodpecker,** a gregarious bird that is close kin to the red-headed woodpecker of forests in the East. Below its red cap it wears a mask from eyes to nape. Dark blue colors its back, wings, and tail. The white patches on its wings show best when it flies, but more white on its brow, chest, rump, and black-streaked underparts make the bird distinctive. So does its habit of storing hundreds of acorns in special holes cut into trees and telephone poles—each acorn hammered securely in place for future use as food. Yet most of its diet is actually insects that bore in dead and dying tree trunks. Its scientific name (*Melanerpes formicivorus*) refers to its liking for carpenter ants.

On the ground below the trees where the acorn woodpecker works, and on slopes still more open to the sky, a fresh display of spring wild flowers attracts hummingbirds that have spent the winter in tropical America. Commonest on the foothills and lower slopes of the Rocky Mountains is the **broad-tailed hummer,** which closely resembles the ruby-throated of the East in having a green cap, back, and mid tail. The outer tail feathers and wing tips are black; the rest of the body is mostly white with a few dark streaks. The male broad-tailed has an iridescent reddish-purple throat which never shows the fiery red of the ruby-throated. The female broad-tailed, who builds the tiny cup-shaped nest and tends her eggs and young alone, lacks the throat color. However, she has orange and white as well as black on her outer tail feathers. In size and markings she is so like a female rufous hummingbird from coastal lowlands that her real identity can be guessed more accurately from the altitude than any other indication besides her choice of mate.

Another look-alike in western mountain country is the female **black-chinned hummer.** She has white tips to her outer tail feathers, which her mate lacks, and closely resembles the female Costa's hummingbird of the desert. She identifies herself by choosing mountain slopes as places to find her mate and build a nest. The male black-chinned is named for the velvety-black chin feathers that develop when he is about one year old. Below the black is a purple stripe of iridescent feathers, but it shows only in good light, appearing black otherwise.

In the same region, the male of the **calliope hummer** is almost always recognizable because special feathers provide purple streaks

Calliope Hummingbird
Stellula calliope
Length 2⅖″ to 3½″

North American Birds

among the white ones on his throat. He can raise the purple feathers separately, but he usually saves this miniature gesture for a potential mate he has in view. He is the smallest bird north of the Mexican boundary, smaller than some moths that visit the same flowers. His tail, and that of his mate, is so short that when he rests, his folded wing tips extend backward beyond his longest tail feather. The female calliope resembles a broad-tailed hummer, but is much smaller and lacks the orange color on her outer tail feathers. Calliopes migrate in summer up the western mountain chains as far as British Columbia.

One level higher up the mountain sides, the trees may be mostly pines, particularly the handsome western yellow (ponderosa) pines that seem specially to appeal to the **pygmy nuthatch.** This little bird is not much bigger than a hummer, but its ecological profession in the mountain community is completely different. At elevations between 3500 and 10,000 feet, it flits from tree to tree, probing for insects in crevices and nesting in knotholes. It clings to the bark while going down, up, or around the tree with equal ease. Agile and vociferous, it repeats its call *KIT-KIT-KIT* almost like a hammer striking metal, sometimes fast enough to become a chatter. It is resident from central Mexico to southern British Columbia, eastward to the farthest foothills of the Rockies. In all of this great area it is the only nuthatch with a grayish-brown cap that comes down to a black mark through the eyes.

Pygmy Nuthatch
Sitta pygmaea
Length 3¾″ to 4¼″

Beyond The Timberline

White-headed woodpeckers make their undulating flights only among the pines and firs in high country of states along the Pacific coast. Males have a small red patch at the nape of the neck, but otherwise the coloring of the two sexes is alike. For some reason that has not yet been discovered, they do not migrate, merely moving up and down slope a short distance according to the season. Perhaps this is

White-Headed Woodpecker
Dendrocopos albolarvatus
Length 9″

North American Birds

why they have not spread to mountain ranges farther east, as **Williamson's sapsuckers** do on their northward trip from the Southwest and Mexico. Almost the only similarity between the male and female of this sapsucker is in the bright yellow underparts. The male bird is otherwise mostly dark blue, with white face stripes and a red chin spot. Splashes of white on rump and wings show conspicuously when he flies. The female has a black chest patch, a brown cap on lighter brown cheeks, and a white rump. Otherwise she is sandy brown, marked transversely with fine dark striping. Both have a call that suggests those of other sapsuckers, but it is drummed in distinctive rhythms—several quick thumps followed by three or four at longer intervals.

Williamson's Sapsucker
Sphyrapicus tyroideus
Length 9½"

Beyond The Timberline

Sometimes you can scarcely hear the sounds of birds on mountain slopes because of a noisy stream tumbling down its rocky channel. This is the place to watch for an inconspicuous little gray bird with short beak, white eye ring, strong yellow legs, and a very short tail. It is the **dipper,** or water ouzel, a year-round resident that never hesitates to walk right into the rushing water and seek insect larvae clinging to the rocks. Often the current sweeps the dipper off its feet; the bird emerges from the torrent and flies around to try again. Whenever it stands to rest, it performs a little curtseying movement like that of a sandpiper, bobbing its entire body up and down. Throughout the year it sings a loud, frequent, bubbling wren-like song. But only in summer does it choose (if possible) a rocky ledge right over the rushing stream and there build its large, roughly spherical nest with a side entrance. Apparently the dipper can find these conditions on mountain sides all the way from central Mexico to Alaska.

Dipper
Cinclus mexicanus
Length 7″ to 8½″

North American Birds

Some birds in high country show a preference for thickets of spruce and fir close to the timber line. It is there you can expect to see spruce grouse in the East and **blue grouse** during winter in the West. Strangely, the blue grouse reverse the common pattern of up-and-down migration, descending into deciduous forests in summer, traveling upward for protection and constantly available food among the evergreens when winter comes. On the down trip, the brownish and bluish gray males put on their courtship displays, producing booming calls as they inflate an orange sac in a whorl of white feathers on each side of the neck. The effect is certainly eye-catching.

The usual schedule of migration is followed by **Clark's nutcracker.** Gray jays without a crest, but with black wings and tail marked with white, in flight they suggest short-tailed mockingbirds. But they are far bolder than most mockingbirds in approaching a human hiker at lunch time, ready to accept nuts or raisins or bread at progressively shorter distances until they are snatching food from an outstretched hand.

Blue Grouse
Dendragapus obscurus
Length 15½″ to 21

Clark's Nutcracker
Nucifraga columbiana
Length 12″ to 13″

Golden-Crowned Sparrow
Zonotrichia atricapilla
Length 6″ to 7″

Harris' Sparrow
Zonotrichia querula
Length 7″ to 7¾″

Beyond The Timberline

The little sparrows of thickets near timber line are far more wary or less interested in the kinds of food man eats. The **golden-crowned sparrow** breeds where the trees are deformed and stunted by the mountain winds, mostly from British Columbia to Alaska. For the winter it comes south and slightly lower near the Pacific coast. **Harris' sparrow** stays east of the Rockies, nesting in the Far North of Canada, and taking winter refuge among thickets in the middle states from the Mississippi River westward to California, Oregon, Washington, and southernmost British Columbia. Both sexes have a pink beak and jet black on crown, face, chin, and throat. Harris' is the continent's largest sparrow. It was named to honor Edward Harris, a friend of John James Audubon who accompanied the artist on his memorable expedition on the Missouri River, helping him both in collecting birds to paint and in getting subscriptions for the *Birds of America*.

Habitually, a few birds go still higher on the mountains, into the alpine tundra beyond the farthest line of upright trees. The **gray-crowned rosy finches** come from their winter wandering over the Great Plains, reaching altitudes between 10,000 and 12,000 feet before selecting a nest site in the lee of a boulder or in a sheltered crevice. They resemble ordinary purple finches with a black forehead and gray cap tied over the crown from eye to eye, but they chirp like house sparrows. The gray-crowneds choose mountains as far south as central California and northwestern Montana, which gives people a chance to meet them in Glacier National Park and the high country of Yosemite and the Sierra Nevada.

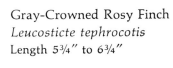

Gray-Crowned Rosy Finch
Leucosticte tephrocotis
Length 5¾″ to 6¾″

North American Birds

Water pipits migrate to the mountain tundras from sea-level wintering sites, and hide their nests among the crags. We recognize these sparrow-sized birds by the way they run along the ground, pausing to pick up food or just to look around. They are forever wagging their white-edged tails up and down. Dissimilar companions—**surfbirds**—often flock with pipits in the Canadian Northwest and Alaska, the surfbirds having migrated from winter feeding grounds along the Pacific coast all the way to mountain tundras in Alaska.

The gray-crowned rosy finches, water pipits, and surfbirds often arrive at their destinations in spring before the snow has melted, and quickly get their nests in order. A late snowstorm may sweep over them while they are still incubating their eggs. Seemingly, at high altitudes and high latitudes, this haste is essential if their young are to reach independence before the growing season comes to its early end.

Surfbird
Aphriza virgata
Length 10"

Beyond The Timberline

Only the **white-tailed ptarmigans** seem well adapted to benefit from short summers and to tolerate long, harsh winters without migrating more than a short distance downslope from the bare tundra near the peak. These birds are an irregular yellowish-brown above during the summer, mottled with white during the fall and spring moulting process, and completely snow white in winter. Only in breeding season does the male have a spot of red atop his head. Ptarmigans match their background superlatively well at any season, and run or crouch rather than take to their wings when danger threatens.

The gusty air of a winter storm is hazardous for any creature. When winds are unpredictable and irresistible, the ptarmigans find safety by burrowing in the snow itself. Despite the cold, they manage to stay warm inside their feathers by frequently dining on fir needles and the exposed buds of alpine willows.

White-Tailed Ptarmigan
Lagopus leucurus
Length 12″ to 13″

North American Birds

Golden eagles cannot manage in this way. They must have meat, alive or dead. Avoiding the worst of the storms, the eagles leave as winter's cold comes on, first from the high latitudes and then from the high altitudes farther south. Unfortunately, during the last century these great birds have died faster than they could reproduce their kind. New man-made dangers they have not yet learned to avoid have brought down their numbers. Soon, they too may be listed among the world's rare and endangered wildlife, threatened with extinction as they come down from their mountain retreats.

CHAPTER SEVEN

THE FAR NORTHERN TUNDRAS

UNTIL WE VISIT A FAR-NORTHERN LAND OR LOFTY MOUNTAIN PEAK, WE CAN scarcely appreciate the good fortune enjoyed by creatures who do not have to struggle with the severity of the polar territories. Actually winds and ocean currents conceal from us a critical shift in temperature that comes at 40 degrees north latitude—along the northern boundary of Kansas and at the approximate latitudes of Reno, Nevada; Denver, Colorado; Dayton, Ohio, and Philadelphia, Pennsylvania. North of this parallel the earth receives from the sun less heat than it radiates again to space. Without air and water convection currents to bring warmth from south of the parallel, the northern land and seas would grow progressively colder until no life could exist.

The effectiveness of such heat redistribution simply becomes inadequate along an irregular boundary extending from northwest Alaska to the middle coast of Labrador. There, climate divides the hardy upright trees from the low tundras stretching on toward the Pole. Despite the long days, the summer is too short and the oblique sun cannot warm the ground enough to thaw the ice below the surface. That surface turns to mud and shallow ponds. Plants grow at a

199

faster rate than seems credible. Small animals reproduce rapidly and become abundant. Migrant birds arrive to benefit from the wealth of food. But soon the nights grow longer, the loss of heat by radiation exceeds the gain from other ways, the water freezes, and the permafrost in the subsoil—unmelted ever since the Ice Ages—is once again renewed.

The willow ptarmigan, which is the state bird of Alaska and the largest of these arctic-alpine birds, is among the few that find enough food and shelter to live on or close to the tundras throughout the year. Even their feet are feathered, as an adaptation for conserving warmth in the winter cold and storms. At most times of year these birds can feed close to where they nest, among whatever scrubby willows, birches, junipers, and heaths that are shielded by solid rock from the bitter winds. The smaller rock ptarmigan chooses slightly higher land where the weather is even more severe. Yet only in small areas of Alaska and the Yukon do these overlap in summer range with the white-tailed ptarmigans, which are common above timber line on mountains as far southward as Colorado. The white-tailed is the only ptarmigan that has no black on the tail and becomes completely white in winter. Rock ptarmigans have a black streak through the eyes and, like the willow ptarmigans, retain black corners on the tail.

The ptarmigans and the snowshoe hares are the largest prey of the **snowy owls,** which float over the snow-covered ground on broad wings stretching nearly five feet tip to tip. Lemmings and other rodents comprise the bulk of each owl's prey, however, and when the periodic crashes occur in these smaller vegetarians' population, the snowy owls often have to fly south or starve. In summer, these big birds remain white and conspicuous. To protect their sensitive golden eyes from the glare of the tundra sun, they raise their cheek and brow feathers until only a horizontal slit remains through which to view their world. Eskimos are credited with following the owls' example in the design of the eye shields they carve from thin bone— each with a horizontal slit to allow vision yet screening the eyes from the glare of sun on snow.

All other tundra birds fly much farther south as soon as their young of the year can make the trip. Mostly they are water and shorebirds. Logically, they come to the tundra to reproduce because

Snowy Owl
Nyctea scandiaca
Length 20″ to 26″

there they can find plenty of space, food in abundance, and comparatively few predators around the myriad ponds and lakes. The space is available because of the breadth of the continent and the small number of permanent residents who could offer competition. The food is there because of the long summer days, a consequence of the tilt of the earth as it rotates and follows its orbit around the sun. The predators are scarce because in winter the tundra can sustain only a limited number of snowy owls, arctic foxes, and scattered packs of wolves. The ponds and lakes, marshes and bogs exist because the great glaciers of the Ice Ages scoured out low basins in the rocks. The permafrost, moreover, tends to block the drainage, letting meltwater stand as long as the humid winds can carry no extra moisture.

The golden eagle follows the smaller birds to the tundras, and so do a few of the streamlined falcons: the gyrfalcon with a 48-inch wing span and the peregrine with a 40-inch. The short-eared owls come north. The lemmings reproduce prodigiously, with all the plant food they can eat. The birds and beasts of prey, eat whenever they have space for another meal and otherwise stand around— ignored by their next victims, who are too numerous to be fearful. Indeed, the most impressive feature of tundra animals in summer is their general lack of wariness.

Even on the almost bare land, the different kinds of birds sort themselves out in choosing nest sites according to slight variations in the landscape. Near the coasts, the quail-sized dovekies seek rocky slopes, cliffs with crevices, and holes between boulders. There each female dovekie lays a single bluish-white egg. When the chick hatches, both parents feed it with regurgitated food from their gleanings of surface plankton from over the cold Arctic waters. Dovekies breed from Ellesmere Island down the coast of Greenland, around Iceland and northernmost Russia, and then fly to open waters of the North Atlantic before ice closes in.

Some of these same bleak, rocky headlands attract also the gull-like **fulmars,** which nest on Canada's arctic islands—around the Pole westward to Alaska and Siberia and eastward to Iceland and northern coasts of the British Isles. Fulmars are tube-nosed birds, close kin to the shearwaters. They often follow ships at sea, feasting on scraps of garbage thrown overboard. Otherwise they skim the ocean

Fulmar
Fulmarus glacialis
Length 17″ to 22″; Wingspread 41″

surface, hunting for small crustaceans, young fishes, and squids. In winter they seek these same morsels southward into the Atlantic Ocean off the coasts of New England and France, and in the Pacific as far as Baja California and Japan.

The driest, stoniest places on lower ground appeal to the plump little **sanderlings,** which line a shallow depression with soft grass or leaves before laying four pear-shaped eggs. Often these preparations are made before the tundra pools have melted enough to hatch any insect larvae. For a while each spring the sanderlings must subsist on small buds and seeds. By mid-August the parents are southbound, leaving their chicks to follow as soon as they are able— usually within the next two weeks. Some of them will fly all the way to the coasts of South America before satisfying their migratory urge. They become familiar to beachcombers as the small plump "peeps" or "whiteys" that follow receding waves and probe the wet sand for minute crustaceans, worms, and mollusks. Although sanderlings are generally sociable in small groups, they seem invariably in a hurry.

Sanderling
Crocethia alba
Length 7″ to 8½″

Less stony tundra that is still dry appeals to both the western sandpipers, which are sparrow-sized peeps, and also the **American golden plovers** that have converged on the arctic tundras from half a world away. For the winter these little sandpipers migrate to coasts from California to Peru and Massachusetts to Venezuela, resting when the tide is high but wading into the waves as it ebbs to snatch at small swimming animals. The golden plovers go much farther, probably traveling nonstop and very high over open water. Those from the tundras of Alaska and Siberia fly to Hawaii, many islands of the South Pacific, Australia, Tasmania, and New Zealand; whereas those from farther east in North America go to South America, spreading out over grasslands from Bolivia and Brazil to Patagonia.

American Golden Plover
Pluvialus dominica
Length 10″ to 11″

Greater Yellowlegs
Totanus melanoleucus
Length 13″ to 15″

The lesser yellowlegs seek drier and more sheltered corners than do the larger **greater yellowlegs.** Both are tall sandpipers with long beaks, gray bodies streaked with brown, and conspicuously long yellow legs which trail behind as the birds fly. They wade about, feeding on insects, other small invertebrate animals, and occasionally a small fish. For the winter they go to the southern United States, chiefly to marsh edges and coastlines, and down through both the West Indies and Central America to as far as the tip of South America.

When they nest, **black-bellied plovers** seem to feel a view of the surroundings is more important than whether the site is dry or moist. The eggs are laid in a little hollowed place, either on bare ground or on a few bits of soft plant material. As soon as the young are independent and finding their own small insects and spiders, crustaceans and snails, earthworms and sea worms, the parents lead the way south. Most of them take the Atlantic or the Pacific flyway to destinations as remote as Brazil or northern Chile.

Black-Bellied Plover
Squatarola squatarola
Length 10½" to 13½"

Snow Bunting
Plectrophenax nivalis
Length 6″ to 7¼″

The Far Northern Tundras

Often the black-bellied plovers have some land birds with a liking for the Far North as their nearest neighbors in the nesting area. Lapland longspurs are often the commonest of summer birds in the Arctic. Their relatives, the **snow buntings,** come oftener to glean bits of food from around human settlements, and have been referred to as the "house sparrows of polar lands." Common redpolls sometimes flock with them until the time of nesting, when each pair of birds finds a sheltered crevice, a concealed thicket between boulders, or a tussock that can accommodate the nest itself. It is made of grasses, lined with hair or fur or feathers according to what the parents can find. During the winter none of these land birds needs to go far south, since they can switch their diet to seeds available in the northern United States and southern Canada as soon as the insects are chilled into inactivity.

In the shelter of rocks or hummocks of vegetation, **water pipits** push the moss aside and make a place for eggs. These little tail-wagging birds are scarcely distinguishable from the other pipits that spend the summer at high elevations. While flying, they undulate like big goldfinches and sing above the nest territory as though they were skylarks. But on the ground, where they forage for small invertebrate animals, they walk, nodding their heads like doves do as they go. With the approach of the arctic winter, the water pipits fly to the coasts and join their kin that have come down from the mountain peaks. Or they find a good place to stay—near an inland marsh or open fields in the southern United States and Mexico—where they can eat well until spring allows them to make the northward migration.

Water Pipit
Anthus spinoletta
Length 6″ to 7″

North American Birds

To moister and often grassy areas of the polar tundra, **black brant** and several kinds of shorebirds regularly make their way each year. The black brant stay in small colonies near open water, each goose incubating her eggs in a grassy nest insulated with plenty of down feathers. Like their kin, the larger Canada geese, black brant are mostly vegetarians. Their favorite food is eelgrass, which grows in shallow coastal water. They offer no competition to the **whimbrels** and **dunlins** which choose similar nest sites, for these shorebirds have completely different feeding habits. The whimbrels use their long curved beaks to get insects from shallow pools of fresh water and to probe for shellfish in coastal mudflats. The dunlins search the Arctic beaches for crustaceans and insects, and peck into the river margins for other small animals.

Black Brant
Branta nigricans
Length 23″ to 26″; Wingspread 45″

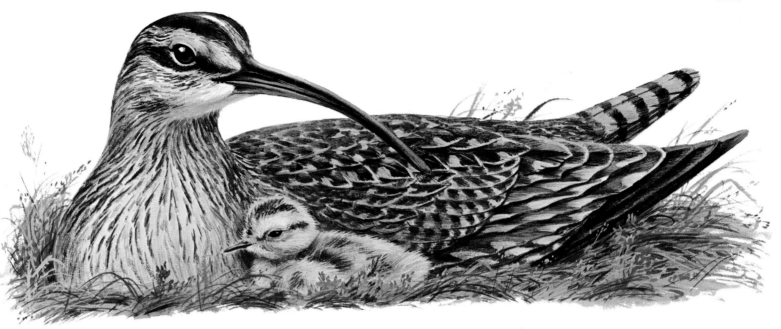

Whimbrel
Numenius phaeopus
Length 15″ to 18″

Dunlin
Erolia alpina
Length 8″ to 9″

North American Birds

The dowitchers and sandpipers sort themselves out in wetter territory. The short-billed dowitcher and the least sandpiper—smallest of all peeps—prefer real muskeg, which is a quaking bog full of peat moss and low shrubs or low trees giving privacy. The **long-billed dowitcher,** like the pectoral and semipalmated sandpipers, go to more open tundra where the view is good. These same sedgy parts of the tundra attract the northern phalaropes, which pick a marshy mound or a tussock where the male of the pair will build the nest and later incubate the eggs his mate lays in it. She does return to help rear the young.

The rare **whooping cranes** choose some of the most remote wet tundra within a hundred miles or so of Great Slave Lake, and carefully build bulky nests of twigs lined with soft vegetation as the place for their two eggs. They have to start early in the polar summer, for their newly hatched young need ten weeks to reach the flying age. Winter is hard on their heels as they start out for their one remaining refuge: the Arkansas National Wildlife Refuge near Rockport, Texas, which has broad marshes along the Gulf of Mexico.

Long-Billed Dowitcher
Limnodromus scolopaceus
Length 11″ to 12½″

Whooping Crane
Grus americana
Length 50″; Wingspread 90″

Black Turnstone
Arenaria melanocephala
Length 9″

Ruddy Turnstone
Arenaria interpres
Length 8″ to 9½″

The Far Northern Tundras

The turnstones seem able to find food other birds miss, merely by looking underneath each clam shell, loose stone, and bit of seaweed. They flick aside lightweight objects by the skillful use of their beaks. Larger stones are shoved bodily: the bird presses its breast against them and heaves. The **black turnstone** lays its eggs in unlined depressions near the edge of tundra pools only along the western and southern coasts of Alaska. The **ruddy turnstone** lines its nest carefully with soft dry grasses and follows this slightly different practice all the way across the American Arctic from Alaska to Greenland. Both kinds of turnstones defend their nests as vigorously as they can, but only the ruddy travels as far as South America for the winter, or has spread its range to Eurasia, Africa, Australia, and islands of the South Pacific.

Inherited differences in nest-building and choice of food reduce competition among related birds with similar distribution. The **arctic loons,** formerly called Pacific loons, limit themselves to the grassy margins of deep lakes of generous size, whereas the red-throated loons accept comparable grassy edges of smaller lakes and also coastal lagoons. Nearness to deep water is doubly important to both kinds of birds, because their legs are so far back on the body that they can scarcely walk on land. Built for deep diving and underwater swimming, they need the deep water as a place for escape and as the source of good-sized fishes for themselves and their young. Both kinds of loons go to the sea coasts farther south for the winter, the red-throateds as far as Florida waters.

Arctic Loon
Gavia arctica
Length 23″ to 29″; Wingspread 40″

North American Birds

The **white-fronted geese** are the only ones with yellow feet and the commonest geese in the western United States. They are circumpolar birds that nest sociably on the tundra, going to open marshes and grassy islands regardless of whether the water around them is salty or brackish or fresh. They are almost wholly vegetarian, and readily accept the smaller berries, grains, fruits, and bits of grass, as though leaving the larger vegetation to the **whistling swans** that often nest near by. The swans, however, also eat crustaceans and mollusks which they reach by extending their long necks downward or tipping their whole bodies tail up. For the winter, the white-fronted geese come down the Pacific flyway to the western United States or down the central flyway to the marshes along the Gulf of Mexico. A few of the whistling swans go to California for the winter, but most cross the continent diagonally, over the Great Lakes to Chesapeake Bay and southward into the coastal Carolinas.

White-Fronted Goose
Anser albifrons
Length 26″ to 34″; Wingspread 58″

Whistling Swan
Olor columbianus
Length 52″; Wingspread 83″

North American Birds

Canada geese—the "honkers" that are so famous for traveling in V formation—and their smaller kin, the **snow geese** and blue geese, are more particular about finding nest sites near freshwater marshes in the tundra. If possible, the Canadas hunt out open marshes and grassy islands for their individual nest, whereas the snows and blues form colonies on barer islands and on wet tundra. Goslings of these geese instinctively choose insects and snails in preference to plant foods that are harder to digest and less nutritious. The goslings grow rapidly and gradually become better able to handle the grasses, roots, seeds, and other vegetable matter their parents eat. As adults, the Canadas make more trouble for grasshoppers than the snows and blues, while the latter two work harder to loosen the roots of plants in marshes and muddy ground as favorite items of diet. For winter, the abundant Canada geese go to coastal and Mississippi Valley states, the snows to more limited stretches of the Pacific, Gulf, and mid-Atlantic coasts, and most of the blues down the Mississippi flyway from their nesting areas near Hudson Bay to marshes around the Gulf of Mexico from New Orleans to Vera Cruz. Since some blues interbreed with snows (and snows with blues) and apparently produce hybrids with intermediate plumage patterns, many birders wonder if these are really separate species.

Canada Goose
Branta canadensis
Length 22″ to 39½″; Wingspread 43½″ to 76″

Snow Goose
Chen hyperborea
Length 29"; Wingspread 58"

Harlequin Duck
Histrionicus histrionicus
Length 14½″ to 21″; Wingspread 25″

The Far Northern Tundras

No such questions apply to the brants, which resemble small Canada geese with all-black heads. They are gregarious and more coastal than most geese, feeding extensively on eelgrass in tide waters. In Eurasia they are known as brent geese. There too they nest in brackish edges of the tundra before migrating south to winter in estuaries along the Atlantic coast from Cape Cod to North Carolina. Until eelgrass was devastated by a disease in the late 1920's, producing a consequently sharp reduction in the brant population, they were the favorite waterfowl of New England hunters.

At the tundra end of the annual migration, the diving ducks sort themselves out in patterns that parallel the geese and shorebirds. **Harlequin ducks,** unable to find hollow logs or tree holes to nest in, settle sociably along streams, preferably near the most rapid water— even a little waterfall. Red-breasted mergansers choose a low place among heather near a river edge, a marsh or lake, or even a bit of tundra where some loose stones give a slight amount of privacy. **Oldsquaws,** whose loud whistling calls often attract attention, accept the shelter of any vegetation for their shallow nests on the ground, but go only where they too are near the water. All of these ducks can dive deeply but do not thrive where they have to do so often. Their food is a mixture of shellfish and small invertebrate animals, plus whatever fishes they can catch in their short, sharp beaks. For the winter, all three of these kinds of diving ducks congregate along Atlantic and Pacific coasts. Some of the oldsquaws and mergansers stay on the Great Lakes where the fresh water stays open even during the coldest weather.

Oldsquaw
Clangula hyemalis
Length 15″ to 22½″; Wingspread 28½″

Only a few kinds of tundra birds remain where the water on every side is salty. Arctic terns lay their eggs and tend their chicks on the most precarious rocky islets, always in dense colonies. Each nest site is just beyond pecking distance of the next one. This habit provides mutual protection against the herring gulls that generally choose to nest colonially on some equally rocky site near by. Although the gulls can scavenge and catch a good many fishes near shore, they are always ready to raid a tern colony for eggs and small chicks. The gulls will fight among themselves over the trophies they manage to snatch before the adult terns repel the invasion.

When the nesting season ends, the gulls need fly only to more southern coasts, to the larger rivers and lakes, and to garbage dumps near human communities. The arctic terns, by contrast, become the world's most inveterate travelers. Those in Alaska join others from Siberian tundras to fly southward along the Pacific coast of the Americas to antarctic waters. Terns from farther east all head for Newfoundland. They cross the North Atlantic to western Europe and the Canary Islands, which is also the rendezvous area for Eurasian members of this species. Together in a vast congregation they travel southward down the African coast. A good many round the Cape of Good Hope and spread out around Madagascar. The rest continue onward past the Antarctic Circle, settling on the sea for relaxation and diving into it for food. These graceful birds, often known as "sea swallows," experience more daylight each year than any other feathered creature. As soon as days on the arctic tundras lengthen again, the arctic terns are back to nest.

Although the terns and gulls catch fishes with apparent ease, they cannot defend themselves and their trophies against the aerial attacks of **parasitic jaegers,** gull-like birds that nest on ledges and bare shores in the vicinity of tern and gull colonies. These winged pirates winter at sea, catching their own food, but become regular robbers of other sea birds when there are jaeger chicks to be fed. The jaegers rely on their own hook-tipped beaks and aerial dexterity to become the aggressors. They force the burdened tern or gull to drop its fish, and then snatch the prize in mid air.

Parasitic Jaeger
Stercorarius parasiticus
Length 16″ to 21″

North American Birds

We wonder whether the common eider ducks and the **surf scoters** that arrive so early in the arctic spring can manage to escape interference from gulls and other predators. They both nest on slopes that may be pebbly or rocky, affording little protection. Eiders congregate with other eiders, gaining security from numbers, but surf scoters are less sociable, relying instead upon a covering of grasses as concealment for the soft down feathers that the mother bird pulls from her breast to shield the eggs from cold. Eider down is perhaps the lightest of heat-retaining materials. Surf scoter down is almost as good, though rarely so thick. The night after their eggs hatch, the mother birds lead their hatchlings to the open water and teach them to dive from danger. While gulls and terns and parasitic jaegers wheel through the sky above, the eider and surf scoters reach for crustaceans and shellfishes in the shallows. The parent birds dine on fishes too, as the young will when they grow larger. Before the arctic tundras grow cold with autumn storms, all of these birds must be off to coastal waters farther south along both Pacific and Atlantic shores.

Surf Scoter
Melanitta perspicillata
Length 17" to 21"; Wingspread 32"

Until man learned to fly faster than any bird, the arctic tundras barred travel between the Old World and the New by the shortest route—over the North Pole. Now that these air distances have gained new appreciation, there is new reason to wonder how distinguishing differences arose among the birds in the two hemispheres. Actually, most birds of the bleak tundras are represented equally in Eurasia and America, although they are often known by somewhat different names—even in English.

American name	European name	American name	European name
Arctic loon	Black-throated diver	Whimbrel	Whimbrel
Red-throated loon	Red-throated diver	Short-billed dowitcher	Red-breasted snipe
Brant	Brent goose	Dunlin	Red-backed sandpiper
White-fronted goose	White-fronted goose	Sanderling	Sanderling
Harlequin duck	Harlequin	Northern phalarope	Red-necked phalarope
Common eider	Eider	Parasitic jaeger	Arctic skua
Oldsquaw	Long-tailed duck	Herring gull	Herring gull
Red-breasted merganser	Red-breasted merganser	Arctic tern	Arctic tern
Gyrfalcon	Gyr falcon	Snowy owl	Snowy owl
Peregrine falcon	Peregrine	Water pipit	Rock pipit
Willow ptarmigan	Willow grouse	Common redpoll	Redpoll
Rock ptarmigan	Ptarmigan	Lapland longspur	Lapland bunting
Black-bellied plover	Gray plover	Snow bunting	Snow bunting

Storms must often sweep migrating birds across narrow portions of the North Atlantic, and less frequently across the greater width of the North Pacific from Asia to America. Vagrants from America turn up rather regularly in the British Isles: snow geese, surf scoters, lesser yellowlegs (known in Europe as yellowshanks), pectoral sandpipers, least sandpipers, and semipalmated sandpipers. Canada geese may arrive in the same way, but would no longer be noticed because a breeding stock introduced some years ago in western Europe has spread widely under wild conditions.

Europe has a native counterpart to our whistling swan in its Bewick's swan, which nests on Eurasian tundras. An Asiatic golden

North American Birds

plover with habits similar to the American golden plover takes the place of ours. The Old World and the New are still distinct. Yet, on the bleak barrens of the polar regions, their similarities and the consequences of past sharing in both directions are particularly prevalent.

CHAPTER EIGHT

SWAMP, STREAM, AND LAKE

To a great many birds, water is more than something to bathe in or to drink. It is a natural lure that appeals to age-old instincts guiding them to food and resting sites. Yet most of the birds that nest close to water discriminate, as we do, between fresh water and salt, between standing and flowing water, but avoid the shore of the sea with its tides and surging waves.

It is not enough to distinguish between land and water birds. These general categories, in fact, are less exclusive than might be thought, largely because birds can show such versatility. The kingfisher nests and perches close to water into which it can dive for food—but does not become thereby a water bird any more than the habits of a human skin-diver make the person a fish.

Water birds and those that come close enough to be called shorebirds have places in eight orders, six of them exclusively related to aquatic habitats. The grebes, with their toes individually webbed, comprise one small order. The loons form another—a group of great antiquity. The tube-nosed birds, such as petrels and albatrosses, are all wanderers over the open oceans that come to land only to reproduce. The swans and geese, ducks and mergansers have an order to themselves and are often spoken of as waterfowl or wildfowl. The pelicans, gannets, and cormorants constitute another order. So do the egrets, herons, bitterns, and ibises.

Marsh birds—such as rails, gallinules, and coots—comprise only a part of the large order to which the grouse and turkey belong. Similarly, an eighth order shows divisions that match the ways of life: the plovers and snipes, sandpipers and phalaropes are called shorebirds, although many of them swim; the gulls and terns and skimmers go together, and often feed or rest along the shore; the auks and murres and puffins are closely related, nesting along the seacoasts and diving for fish in salt water.

In North America, the birds of fresh waters are particularly widespread, if only because our continent has so much fresh water. Half of the 30 largest lakes in the world and an incredible number of smaller ones must be counted among this bounty. Most of them are in forest land, where the glaciers of the Ice Ages scoured pockets in the rock. Lake Superior is the largest freshwater lake of all. It and the four other Great Lakes along the border between the United States and Canada contain among them more than a fourth of all the fresh water held by lakes and rivers on the planet. This water enters from streams and wetlands that have no match elsewhere, despite the fact that North America does not have the largest river (the Amazon), the second largest (the Congo), or the longest (the Nile). The birds on this one-twentieth of the world's land surface can use as nest sites and feeding areas more marshlands, more stream edges, more swamps, and more lake shores than are available in comparable space on any other continent.

Fully a third of the bird species that frequent the fresh waters of the United States and Canada choose their nest sites on the ground or in shrubbery close to the water's edge. The grebes go a step further, building floating nests from reeds and other marsh vegetation—little private islands that rise and fall with the water level, keeping the eggs dry. Largest of these short-tailed birds are the **western grebes,** with a 40-inch wing span. They breed in colonies from far north in the prairie provinces of Canada to the Pacific coast, wintering inland if the water stays open but otherwise in tidal shal-

Western Grebe
Aechmophorus occidentalis
Length 22″ to 29″; Wingspread 30″ to 40″

North American Birds

lows from British Columbia to Mexico. The small, **eared grebes** of the western states are sociable nesters too, generally in shallow water; most go to inland Mexico for the winter. **Pied-billed grebes** of about the same size range widely, coast to coast. From the Gulf of Mexico to Hudson Bay, they seek out solitary sites to nest. Except in migration to open waters farther south in winter, they seldom fly. Like all grebes, they are expert divers, starting in within minutes after hatching from the egg, pursuing and catching water beetles, crayfish, and other crustaceans, and even outswimming small fishes in their own environment.

Eared Grebe
Podiceps caspicus
Length 12″ to 14″; Wingspread 22½″

Pied-Billed Grebe
Podilymbus podiceps
Length 13″; Wingspread 23″

North American Birds

Commonest of the grebes in the Northwest and the East—where it travels both the Atlantic and the Mississippi flyways to winter in flocks along the coast—is the **horned grebe.** It nests in the marshy margins of ponds and lakes. As is usual among birds of this order, both parents attend the two to seven young. Often one adult bird dives for food and brings it back, while the little birds ride pickaback on the other parent.

Horned Grebe
Podiceps auritus
Length 13″; Wingspread 24″

Swamp, Stream, And Lake

West of the Great Lakes and of Arkansas, the little **ruddy ducks** act in many ways as though they were grebes. They build floating nests among the reeds, dive for small animals to eat in shallow water, and even sink themselves gradually when wanting to be inconspicuous. But they are actually chunky ducks with a flattened beak and stiff, stubby tail which often is held at a jaunty angle. For the winter, they migrate to the West Coast and Mexico, to the southeastern states and West Indies, congregating particularly in Puerto Rico.

Ruddy Duck
Oxyura jamaicensis
Length 14½″ to 16″; Wingspread 22½″

Canvasback
Aythya valisineria
Length 21″; Wingspread 33″

Swamp, Stream, And Lake

A natural island, no matter how small, appeals to a duck nearly twice the size—the **canvasback**—or to an American avocet, or to a trumpeter swan, providing the geographical location is right. Canvasbacks find conditions right from central Alaska to New Mexico, and east to Wisconsin. Eating mostly water plants, they raise their young and then take wing, often flying in V formation like geese. Some cross the continent southeastward to enter the Atlantic flyway and winter in tidewater along the coast. Others take the more western flyways to the Gulf of Mexico, the Pacific shoreline, and even well down in Mexico wherever they can find marshy lakes in which to feed. **Avocets** rarely come east of the Mississippi, but nest from eastern California to the prairie sloughs of central Canada, even along the shores of alkaline lakes. Wading rapidly on their long legs in the shallows, they swish their slender upcurved beaks from side to side, catching water insects, crustaceans, mollusks, and small worms, even taking some seeds of the right sizes and kinds. By autumn they are southbound, chiefly to wetlands of Mexico and Guatemala, although a few turn up in southern Florida and quite a number on irrigated fields in southwestern California. Since they catch insects and rarely touch crops, avocets are generally welcomed as well as admired. Not everyone realizes that the male builds the nest and makes it fit his smaller mate.

Avocet
Recurvirostra americana
Length 15½" to 20"

North American Birds

Trumpeter swans, our heaviest flying birds, may have a wing span of eight feet. Before 1700 A.D., they were apparently numerous and nested from the Pacific coast of British Columbia to northern Missouri and western Quebec; they migrated for the winter to Delaware Bay, the eastern shores of Virginia, the Gulf coasts of Texas and Louisiana, the lower Mississippi River, and various areas in California, the Columbia River basin, Puget Sound, and western British Columbia. By 1932, less than 70 of these swans remained in the United States. All of them had lost the migratory urge and huddled, instead, on some little lakes near the junction of Idaho, Wyoming, and Montana, where a generous outflow of hot water from thermal springs kept ice from forming even during the coldest winter. Given protection in Yellowstone National Park, Jackson Hole National Monument, Wyoming, and Red Rock Lakes National Wildlife Refuge in Montana, the population has increased to more than 600 birds. Somewhat larger wild populations still migrate from nesting areas in coastal southern Alaska and western Alberta to an extensive wintering range along the shores of British Columbia, including all of Puget Sound.

While looking for trumpeter swans in summer, in the same area we have found **white pelicans** with an even greater wing span—to more than nine feet. But these are far lighter birds and can soar

Trumpeter Swan
Olor buccinator
Length 58½″ to 72″; Wingspread 100″

White Pelican
Pelecanus erythrorhynchos
Length 54″ to 70″; Wingspread 100″

North American Birds

spectacularly on outstretched pinions. They nest colonially on bare islands in shallow water. From western Manitoba across British Columbia and Nevada to the Pacific coast, their seclusion is often temporary. As summer drought lowers the level of the lake, predators test the shallows repeatedly to see if the time has come to wade across and feast on young pelicans. The parent birds stuff their young with regurgitated fish, speeding growth toward the day when the nestlings can hobble awkwardly to the water and swim away from danger. Many are lost before the remaining young take off with their parents to fly south to the Gulf coast and Mexico and adjacent waters in California. There they generally join nonbreeding white pelicans that have not yet left the wintering areas—not yet old enough to share in reproducing their kind and fending off all others.

Sometimes the **common terns** share an island with white pelicans in the Canadian prairie provinces. These graceful "sea swallows" are more at home on fresh water than along the coasts, although their nesting range extends from the Yukon across the Great Lakes to

Common Tern
Sterna hirundo
Length 13″ to 16″

Newfoundland and Labrador, south along the Atlantic coast to Georgia. We avoid visiting their nest sites during the breeding season, because when the parent birds are frightened away, gulls take a heavy toll of eggs and chicks. Common terns winter along Pacific coasts from Mexico to Ecuador, and from Florida around the Gulf of Mexico, down the Atlantic side of South America to Patagonia. Near the surface of salt water or fresh, they seem able to find two-inch fishes to dive for and reach their targets more than half the time.

The sloughs and potholes of the prairie provinces are part of a broad pattern of freshwater marshlands that sportsmen sometimes refer to as "America's duck factory." The biggest production is of **mallards**—adaptable ducks that combine insects and vegetable matter in their diet, feeding at the surface just as they do over so much

Mallard
Anas platyrhynchos
Length 22½"; Wingspread 36"

Lesser Scaup
Aythya affinis
Length 15″ to 18½″; Wingspread 27½″

Swamp, Stream, And Lake

of the Old World. Before winter they take themselves south along all of the flyways, a few traveling as far as Panama, the East Indies, India, and South Africa. In North America's southern marshlands, river edges, and estuaries they often spend the cold months sociably flocking with lesser scaups and pintails whose nesting range is almost identical, and with black ducks from eastern Canada and adjacent states. **Lesser scaups** sometimes nest beside a muskrat tunnel opening, into which they can dive and swim away unseen under water if danger threatens. **Pintails** tend to nest in the grass; as dabbling ducks, they cannot escape like a submarine. A pair of black ducks will elevate their grassy, down-lined nursery on a low rotting stump if they can find one.

Pintail
Anas acuta
Length 21½″ to 27″; Wingspread 34″

American Widgeon
Mareca americana
Length 19½″; Wingspread 32½″

Swamp, Stream, And Lake

Some of our commonest ducks show amazing differences in their choice of nest sites. The gadwall of the West hides herself among the reeds, while in many of the same regions the **American widgeon** —often called the baldpate—nests on dry ground, casually concealed or open to the sky, and manages just as well. **Redheads** prepare their nests in tufts of grass so close to the stream or pond that the combined weight of eggs and parent often threatens to topple all together into the water. The ring-necked duck, which is even more conspicuously ring-billed, seems equally intent on nesting among dense vegetation in the border of the pool or lake. But by accepting sites near alkaline or salty water as well as fresh, it does not limit its distribution the way the redhead does. The ring-necked can breed across Canada and south through Utah into northern Arizona, next to forest, to desert, to plains, and to open sea.

Redhead
Aythya americana
Length 18″ to 22″; Wingspread 32″

North American Birds

We might conclude that a short trip from nest to water was important in the survival of the newly hatched ducklings if not for the fact that the abundant mallards seem equally successful when they choose a nest site well back from a pond or stream as when they nest close by. **Shovelers** too often nest quite a distance from the water, and their young make the hazardous trip overland in most of North America except for the East and South. From coast to coast the blue-winged teal and **green-winged teal** show similar unconcern over distance from the water. So do cinnamon teal in the West. Most of these ducks spend the winter in the southern United States and Mexico. Many travel across the West Indies to northern South America, or follow the route through Central America to Panama and beyond.

Shoveler
Spatula clypeata
Length 17″ to 20″; Wingspread 31″

Green-Winged Teal
Anas carolinensis
Length 14″; Wingspread 23″

North American Birds

When we visit these migrants far south, we see them resting and feeding while winter grips their nesting territories in the northern United States and Canada. As a general rule, they wait until the season is right for them to fly north again, making no attempt to raise a family at both ends of their annual trip. On their northern grounds they may efficiently produce several broods in sequence. But their heritage and surroundings in the South call for taking no advantage of summer in both hemispheres. Any northern nester that does remain at the winter address and nest there becomes a special event, worth a place in the newspaper and perhaps a scientific report as well. The bird might become an immigrant instead of a seasonal visitor.

Cinnamon teal are among the few that have developed a regular schedule of nesting in South America. Long ago a flock of these birds may have flown too far south and begun responding to new clues from their strange environment. The intriguing fact is that today the separate populations move synchronously and in the same direc-

Cinnamon Teal
Anas cyanoptera
Length 14½″ to 17; Wingspread 24½″

tions, although with different activities ahead. When the goals are to the south, the birds from western Canada and the United States are ready to wait out the winter in Mexico and as far as northern South America; the teal that have been resting in Peru, Bolivia, and southernmost Brazil are on their way to nest on the pampas of Argentina and in Patagonia. When these birds of the Southern Hemisphere travel with their young of the year to their resting grounds part way north on the same continent, the North American population is on its way toward the Canadian border and across it. Scientists wonder how long it will be before these two populations evolve into independent species.

Unless we see waterfowl on migration, when they are in flocks and alight or take off conspicuously on open water, we are apt to overlook their presence. Wherever they stay a while, whether in their nesting area or their winter territory, they tend to be wary and elusive. Several pairs, in fact, can be at home in a small marsh where the only obvious birds are the males of the common **red-wing.**

Red-winged Blackbird
Agelaius phoeniceus
Length 7½″ to 9½″

North American Birds

Male redwings arrive from their winter quarters and vocally stake out their claims to definite areas in freshwater marshes from Mexico to the Canadian Northwest Territories, British Columbia and California to Nova Scotia and Florida. About a week later, when the boundary lines have been fairly well agreed upon, their mates appear—like big brown sparrows heavily marked with dark spots and streaks. While the male perches in plain sight, calling *gurgle-eee-ee*, spreading his tail and the red-and-gold epaulets on his shoulders, she builds her nest among the cattails or on a low branch overhanging the water. In California, the very similar **tricolored blackbird** behaves in like manner, often in dense crowds among the stands of western bulrushes known as tules. The male tricolor has a white edge, instead of a gold one, to the red patch on his shoulder, and his song seems harsh, with none of the musical quality of the more widespread common redwing.

West of the Mississippi, the larger **yellow-headed blackbirds** often make themselves at home in the same cattail and tule marshes, taking sites the redwings might otherwise occupy. Male yellow-headeds fly more heavily and display white patches on their wings as well as the golden yellow of their heads and throats. Females are usually too busy nest-building, incubating, and feeding offspring to show their golden yellow breasts and the streaked white area of their underparts.

Tricolored Blackbird
Agelaius tricolor
Length 7½″ to 9″

Yellow-Headed Blackbird
Xanthocephalus xanthocephalus
Length 9″ to 11″

North American Birds

Hidden in the same marsh over which the male redwings preside are many other birds, some smaller, some larger, but all less likely to show themselves more than is necessary while finding food. Across all but the southern United States and northward into Canada, the long-billed marsh wren builds ball-shaped nests of grasses attached to the reeds. Often the males pop in and out of the side entrances in the dummy nests they erect, singing by day and sometimes by night too, but producing songs so rattly and guttural that people mistake them for insect sounds. The females slip in and out from the real nests, usually making no sound at all.

Only when the marsh has been silent and undisturbed, except for the calls of birds and frogs, will a male bittern begin his hollow-sounding two-note song. Chaucer claimed the bird "bumbleth in the mire." Country folk have compared the sound of the **American bittern** with that of a hand-operated pump on a well, *PUMP-a-DUMP*, *PUMP-a-DUMP*. At the slightest disturbance, the bird stands perfectly still, its beak pointing at the sky. In this position the brown streaks on the under feathers match the pattern of the reeds, and the bird's eyes give it panoramic vision. The female bittern too sits head up on her low nest of vegetation, hidden among the rushes and cattails, its bottom barely above water.

The commonest of the plump little rails, the **sora,** is rarely seen. If surprised, it may fly a short distance and then run away. Yet it does travel twice a year for 2000 miles or more, wintering in the Gulf States, the West Indies, and Latin America but nesting across the northern United States and Canada. Feeding on insects and many kinds of seeds, it both supports and conceals its nest among

American Bittern
Botaurus lentiginosus
Length 27"; Wingspread 39"

Sora
Porzana carolina
Length 8″ to 9¾″

Common Gallinule
Gallinula chloropus
Length 12″ to 14½″

tall grasses or sedges or cattails. Equally reluctant to fly, but willing to run or swim to sanctuary, are the larger **common gallinules** and coots. This gallinule, formerly known as the Florida gallinule, winters around the Gulf of Mexico and well down into Central America, then flies to nesting territories in California and in states east of the Mississippi north to the Quebec border. The **American coot,** often called a mud hen, even nests in loose colonies without disclosing the site of its nest, hidden among vegetation near the water. It finds suitable places over a great part of the continent, from Nicaragua north to New Brunswick and British Columbia. Numbers of these birds winter in sociable groups along southern coasts and up the Mississippi valley. They may give a false impression of greater abundance to the observer who forgets that in summer they spread out over a vast area of the continent.

American Coot
Fulica americana
Length 13″ to 16″

North American Birds

A few of the land birds of sparrow size take advantage of the marshy borders in nesting season. The **northern waterthrush** gathers soft mosses and builds a deep cup at the base of an alder or some other tree at the water's edge. Actually the bird is a wood warbler whose shape and streaked breast, washed with yellow, show it to be a close kin to the ovenbird. It walks sedately along the muddy margins looking for insects, teetering now and then like a sandpiper, occasionally raising its voice in a clear, loud song that begins in one key and then drops slightly in pitch: *HUR-RY, HUR-RY, HUR-RY, pretty, pretty, pretty, pretty.* The swamp sparrows in the same marshes sound like chipping sparrows singing at slow speed. The swamp sparrow's chestnut cap is narrower, its tail rounded instead of forked like that of a chipping sparrow, and its nest is a saucer-shaped nursery built of grass in some tangled stand of rushes or sedges.

Northern Waterthrush
Seiurus noveboracensis
Length 5″ to 6″

Swamp, Stream, And Lake

A surprising number of American birds don't seem to care whether water is fresh, brackish, salt, or alkaline. This explains why so many "sea gulls"—actually **California gulls**—were so promptly on hand in 1848 to eat up the crickets that plagued the Mormon pioneers along the west side of Great Salt Lake. Although the birds seemed to arrive through the intervention of Divine Providence, they normally include "Mormon crickets" as part of their diet— over the great part of the West where the crickets are available. Now the state bird of Utah and represented in Salt Lake City atop a monument, the California gull continues to nest in close proximity to others of its kind as well as near great blue herons, double-crested cormorants, and white pelicans, on shores and islands around Great Salt Lake. The gulls' range extends from northeastern California to northwestern North Dakota, north into the Canadian prairie provinces. Over this area they glean insects, small rodents, fish, and other aquatic animals in shallow water, as well as whatever garbage they can find.

California Gull
Larus californicus
Length 20" to 23"

Laughing gulls—with a similarly catholic taste in foods and tolerance for waters of high or low mineral content—are much more widespread. Often they nest close to gull-like Caspian terns on bare beaches of sand or gravel, although they are equally capable of building reasonably good saucers of soft grasses to hold their eggs. Similarly, the Caspian terns can dive quite well for fish, but seldom miss an opportunity to rob other birds of their eggs.

Many of these eggs and downy young as well are in plain sight amid the litter of debris on beaches and dunes near the water. It is there that the semipalmated and piping plovers raise their families, with no trace of nesting materials to give away the position of their chocolate-spotted eggs. To us the semipalmated plover suggests a killdeer with one neck band instead of two. Its two-part whistle ascends the musical scale, whereas that of the piping plover descends, becoming one mournful sea coast sound that can be heard inland as well. A male piping plover has a narrow neck band, too, but the paleness of his head and body gives him a wraith-like ability to appear and disappear in full sunlight, according to whether he moves or stands still.

One of the medium-sized shorebirds, the willet, divides its wintering population on salt marshes into a western group that go to freshwater lakes and prairie potholes where they nest among cattails and tules, and an eastern contingent that stays near the sea, raising young in salt marshes. The western willets keep company in summer with **black terns,** the willets wading in shallow water while snatching insects and crustaceans, the terns hovering and picking insects from the surface of deeper water or catching slow-flying kinds on the wing. The young willets soon accompany their parents and find their own food, whereas the terns must continue for much of the summer to feed their flightless chicks by regurgitation—finding the right little bird wherever it has wandered amid the colony in the marsh.

Laughing Gull
Larus atricilla
Length 15½" to 17"

Black Tern
Chlidonias niger
Length 9″ to 10¼″

North American Birds

Black terns, which are the darkest colored of all terns widespread in interior North America, are almost exclusively freshwater birds at breeding season. The **gull-billed terns,** which are the whitest of terns along the coast, are less critical and often fly inland. Both terns depend upon insects for food, rarely diving after a fish no matter how close to the surface it swims. Instead, the terns hawk over the marsh vegetation and dive frequently to catch grasshoppers.

Gull-Billed Tern
Gelochelidon nilotica
Length 18″ to 21″

Swamp, Stream, And Lake

The narrow pointed wings and constant motion of the terns distinguish them even at a distance from **marsh hawks** which soar and tilt and often hover over the marshes. The broader wings of the hawk have feathers extending like fingers at the tips and may span 3½ feet —seven inches more than the spread of either tern. This widespread hawk, equally ready to nest on the ground in the midst of the marsh or on the prairie, takes larger prey: young muskrats and other mammals, small birds, and the biggest insects the wetlands can produce. Its versatility seems to give it freedom to harry for food more widely than any other hawk in North America.

Marsh Hawk
Circus cyaneus
Length 18″ to 24″; Wingspread 42″ to 49″

North American Birds

In the South and West, the approach of a marsh hawk or innocent bird-watcher is likely to cause a great outcry from **black-necked stilts,** which nest singly or in small groups on the ground among the weeds. The back and wings of a stilt are black, as well as the back of its neck and top of its head. These birds wade actively on unbelievably long legs, using their upcurved slender beaks to peck vigorously at snails, crustaceans, insects, and other tidbits of the shallows. Unlike their close kin, the avocets, they never seem to swish their beaks from side to side.

The same kinds of food and similar nest sites on moist ground near water have appeal for larger shorebirds with downcurved, instead of upcurved, beaks. Both the long-billed curlews of the West and the whimbrels—formerly called Hudsonian curlews—of the Far North cry *KER-LEW*. But the long-billeds make this whistle a loud question, rising in pitch at the end, whereas the whimbrels keep the tone softer and more uniform. Their voice is familiar in Eurasia as well as throughout the Americas. For winter, the whimbrels go down both coasts of South America, whereas the long-billed curlews stop when they reach Mexico and Central America.

Almost every summer, no matter where we are in the United States and Canada, we accidentally disturb a **spotted sandpiper** nesting a hundred yards or more from water in some moist meadow.

Spotted Sandpiper
Actitis macularia
Length 7″ to 8″

Black-Necked Stilt
Himantopus mexicanus
Length 13″ to 17″

Common Snipe
Capella gallinago
Length 10½″ to 11½″

The bird flies off but quickly alights near by, teeters nervously, and pipes in a shrill voice to distract us from her eggs or downy young. More often we see these birds on errands of their own, alighting on the margin of a pond, the lip of a dam over which a trickle of water flows, or a floating log to teeter and then pick up an insect. Occasionally the spotted sandpiper dives and swims underwater while pursuing an active beetle.

Somewhat closer to a stream or swamp, where the soil is damp all summer, if we walk through the ferns and mosses we are likely to flush a **common snipe,** causing it to dash off on short wings, taking a zigzag course through the nearest trees, crying *ES-CAPE, ES-CAPE* and not *"a snipe, a snipe"*—as we might guess from its name. This long-billed bird probes the moist soil for earthworms, insects, and other small animals, and generally makes a simple nest on a low mound in the shade. Known by many hunters as a jacksnipe or as Wilson's snipe, these widespread birds in America are but part of a circumpolar population with representatives across Eurasia as well. Their closest kin on American soil are the **woodcocks** which are such masters of camouflage. Just occasionally we discover a woodcock

Woodcock
Philohela minor
Length 10″ to 12″

North American Birds

motionless on her eggs in an open field. Generally the bird moves no muscle as we approach within touching distance—except, perhaps, for a slight parting of the long, straight beak and a hint of panting movements in the throat. Almost always the woodcock nest is fairly close to an alder swamp into which the mother can lead her young as soon as they hatch. Certainly from the field the female woodcock can watch her mate as he performs his aerial courtship dance at twilight. He spirals on strangely whistling wings before plunging through the semi-dark to the ground at her side.

Some of the colonial water birds perch in the shrubbery and low trees near the water while they go through their repertory of courtship gestures. Later they build their nests in the same place. A male of the **common egret** has about 50 especially handsome feathers on his back at mating time, enhancing his display. To get these plumes for the millinery trade, hunters almost exterminated these egrets in the early years of the twentieth century. At least one warden of a bird sanctuary lost his life trying to protect them from poachers. Now recovered in numbers, the common egrets are accepted as "white herons" that stand beside open water, waiting to stab a passing fish or frog. Posed so conspicuously, the bird shows its black legs, feet, and beak tip, its uniformly white feathers, and the butter-yellow on most of its beak. By contrast, the smaller **snowy egret** is usually dashing about in pursuit of insects and little fishes. More southern in distribution, it has yellow feet and a black beak with yellow or red skin at the base.

Common Egret
Casmerodius albus
Length 39"; Wingspread 55"

Snowy Egret
Leucophoyx thula
Length 24″; Wingspread 38″

Green Heron
Butorides virescens
Length 18″; Wingspread 25″

Swamp, Stream, And Lake

The smallest of the heron tribe, the **green heron,** and the most stocky in body build, the **black-crowned night heron,** may nest in solitude or in a rookery with others of their kind. They build platforms of dry twigs to hold their eggs and young, sometimes close to the ground and near a stream, but frequently at a distance as great as a quarter of a mile and higher up. The little green often appears more blue than green, and black at a distance. It patrols the smallest ditches, the most twisting creeks, mostly feeding early and late in the day on an almost endless variety of animal food: fish, frogs, insects, worms, snakes, and even mice. The night herons, often known as "quowks" from the calls they produce while flying from the roost trees to fishing territories, are abroad mostly at twilight. Yet, throughout most of the world's Tropics and temperate regions, they are quick enough to catch a fish or a dragonfly and ready to eat carrion they notice drifting with the current.

Black-Crowned Night Heron
Nycticorax nycticorax
Length 25"; Wingspread 44"

North American Birds

The longer downcurved beak and more slender neck of the ibises help us know these slightly larger birds in a rookery. In the American Southwest, the ibis is the **white-faced,** which in breeding season wears its distinctive marking close to the beak. At other seasons it is almost indistinguishable from the glossy ibis, a widespread bird that nests around the Gulf of Mexico from Texas to Florida, down through the West Indies, across southern Eurasia, Africa, Madagascar, and Australia—wandering occasionally as far as New Zealand but not yet breeding there.

The **wood ibis** of freshwater wetlands in southern Florida and southward to central Argentina and Peru, is actually a stork—the only true stork in the New World. Probably it is a bird of the Southern Hemisphere that stays in time with its formerly exclusive homelands, for in Florida it nests between December and March, surrounded by wintering waterfowl from farther north. The wood

White-Faced Ibis
Plegadis chihi
Length 19″ to 26″; Wingspread 38″

Wood Ibis
Mycteria americana
Length 41″; Wingspread 65″

ibises in the Tropics and in temperate South America nest at this same period, which is summer south of the Tropic of Capricorn. In our spring, the young wood ibises and adults often wander widely to California and eastern Canada, as well as to points in between. But though there are plenty of frogs and fishes, crayfishes and other small animals to eat in these temperate parts of the Northern Hemisphere, they are not available during the season that wood ibises choose to nest. No other feature of the environment seems to limit these storks to breeding in the Everglades. Some day they may switch their inner clocks and begin to spread spectacularly.

The bushes and low trees in which egrets, ibises, and the small herons nest are also homes for smaller birds that like to raise their young near the water. The Virginia rail chooses a site in the dense vegetation, gathering soft weeds to build a cup that is wonderfully concealed. Apparently this shy bird eats a larger proportion of seeds and fewer small animals than its close relatives. While searching for this mixed diet, it squeaks and chirps and grunts in such a variety of calls that it sounds like a dozen different birds at once.

Far easier to recognize by sound and sight are the little warblers of the swamps—the **yellowthroats**—and the widespread song sparrows. These birds repeat their characteristic songs so often that they become theme-singers for the shrubby wetland habitat. The loud *WITCHITY-WITCHITY-WITCH* of the yellowthroat helps us locate the bird as it dodges among the foliage, hunting for insects. Its deep, bulky nest is hard to find among the underbrush, for it is constructed of such a miscellany of dry leaves, grasses, fibrous roots, and lengths of hair that it seems to be some kind of trashpile assembled by sheer chance. The song sparrow builds a simpler cup of grasses and weeds, lining it with fine fibers. These birds are nesters, migrants, or winter visitors in every state south of the Canadian border, and spread north into Canada as well each summer. The song sparrows sing their territorial refrains as far northwest as coastal Alaska, and from Georgia to Labrador. Generally the first few to arrive on a marsh in spring are taken as a sure sign that the welcome season has at last arrived.

In the American Southwest, we can be equally delighted to be on hand when the vermilion flycatchers come north out of Mexico. Sparrow-sized, they perch on wires and on bare tree branches, particu-

Swamp, Stream, And Lake

larly near some irrigation ditch or stream where more insects will be flying. The red cap and throat and underparts of the male make him recognizable from a great distance. His mate has a dark cap and is pale below, her sides finely streaked and her flanks a strawberry pink. She chooses a horizontal fork in a branch of a mesquite, scrub oak, or some other tree near the water and builds a shallow cup with plant fibers, lining it with feathers and hair. After the breeding season, vermilions wander wherever they find insects, occasionally as far as southern Florida. But when cold weather arrives, they fly south into the Tropics where most live permanently.

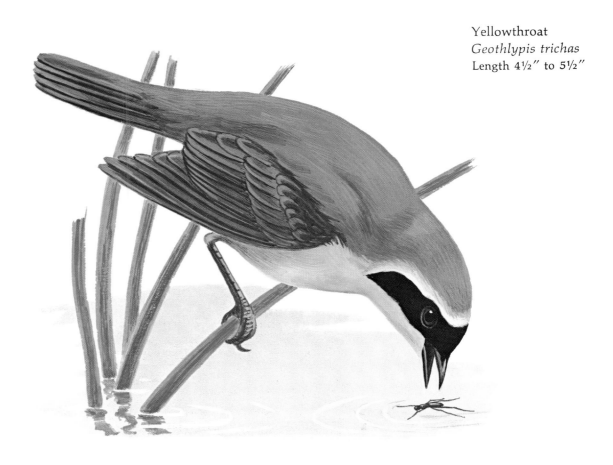

Yellowthroat
Geothlypis trichas
Length 4½″ to 5½″

North American Birds

In a swamp or around the edge of a marsh, the flying birds have no more difficulty than usual in reaching the top of tall trees, but certainly the nest sites they choose reflect an apparent indifference to altitude. The first summer we spent in western Wyoming we discovered Canada geese nesting in trees; we had always previously seen these birds raising their families on the ground. Herring gulls too build high nests in some parts of the continent, but seem just as much at home in others on bald promontories or bare islands. The **ring-billed gulls,** which are commoner inland than along the coast, scavenge the water margins and hunt grasshoppers. Their nestlings are as happy in a tree as in a nest on the ground, where the young birds have nowhere to fall if they slip over the side. Perhaps the most opportunistic bird we have studied is the solitary sandpiper, which teeters its head instead of its tail. It lets other birds house their families and then takes over their abandoned nests. At almost any height, it will take its accommodations second-hand from a grackle, a jay, or a robin.

Ring-Billed Gull
Larus delawarensis
Length 18" to 20"; Wingspread 48"

Double-crested cormorants are almost equally versatile, constructing their crude saucers of sticks and stiff herbs almost anywhere on open ground, ledges of precipitous cliffs, tall trees, or low bushes. Proximity to good fishing waters is more important. They find the right combination well inland and north into the prairie provinces of Canada. For the winter these big birds migrate to the coasts and the shores of southern rivers, such as the Mississippi and the Rio Grande. Everywhere they dive from the surface for fish, gulping their prey whole after rising for air and pointing their hook-tipped beaks to the sky. In this position, gravity helps propel the fish into the bird's crop.

Double-Crested Cormorant
Phalacrocorax auritus
Length 32″; Wingspread 51″

Great Blue Heron
Ardea herodias
Length 46"; Wingspread 70"

Swamp, Stream, And Lake

In the southern and southeastern states, we have to be critical of beak shape if we are to distinguish the cormorants from the similar **anhingas,** which have a straight, tapering, sharp-pointed beak and fish in the same way. Both of these birds have poor oil glands, and their feathers get wet while they swim under water. Afterward, they spend hours with their wings spread to dry again in the sun.

With a wing span as much as 80 inches, a **great blue heron** can come readily to its nest either on the ground or in the top of a tree 150 feet high. Often these birds have to allow for a breeze that

Anhinga
Anhinga anhinga
Length 34″; Wingspread 48″

is shaking the treetop even as they try to alight at the nest—which argues for the benefits of choosing a lower site. These birds show great patience, standing in shallow fresh water or salty lagoon, waiting for an unwary fish or frog to swim near enough to be caught by a sudden stabbing motion of the long, sharp beak. Great blues eat also many other kinds of food that comes their way: small crabs, large grasshoppers, water snakes, swimming mice and shrews. On a mixed diet these birds range from Alaska and the maritime provinces of Canada south into Central America.

The distribution and population of some other big birds that nest in trees near fresh water have shrunk dangerously. Some of the declines can be traced to alterations in their environment. The magnificent ivory-billed woodpecker vanished from southern Florida when the tall bald-cypress trees were felled to make lumber, leaving few nest sites and a scarcity of dead wood into which to drill for insects. The **bald eagles** that once were numerous and widespread and the **ospreys** that fished over so much of the continent are now uncommon and local. Dangerous chemicals now taint the live fishes the ospreys catch and the dead ones upon which eagles feast. The birds accumulate the poisons until their reproductive systems falter. We used to find eagle nests in tall pines, and ospreys sharing food with their young on eyries built atop the crossbars of telephone poles and the roofs of boathouses. Many of the trees and roofs still stand, but the birds are gone.

From the Tropics and South America, the kites now come less frequently to the United States than they used to because so many of the wetlands have been drained, the forests felled, and the kites themselves shot by hunters who regard any member of the hawk clan as vermin. Most graceful and trusting still are the **swallow-tailed kites,** which dart and hover, climb and dive over marshes and swamp forests in the Gulf States. Once fairly common as breeding birds in most of the East, as nesters they are now restricted to the Florida Everglades. They are particularly active in early morning and late afternoon. Spreading wide their deeply divided swallow tails, they seem to hang in the air before sinking smartly with wings upraised and feet downstretched to grasp some grasshopper, snake, or frog. Rising rapidly with their prey, they eat it on the wing and then search for another. But before Christmas comes, all swallow-tailed

Bald Eagle
Haliaetus leucocephalus
Length 34″ to 36″; Wingspread 80″ to 85″

Osprey
Pandion haliaetus
Length 23″; Wingspread 68″

Swallow-Tailed Kite
Elanoides forficatus
Length 24"; Wingspread 48"

North American Birds

kites depart for wetlands farther south. Their range extends to Argentina. Even in Mexico, most kites of this kind are migrants that come north for the summer season only.

A **white-tailed kite,** with a broad white tail, can be mistaken for a gull. Its mode of hunting is the same, but its prey usually is a mouse or other small mammal. White-taileds soar when the wind is strong, and show little tendency to migrate. Fortunately they are still numerous from Central America to Chile, for in Mexico few are left and in the United States they are rarities recorded from western California, southeastern Texas, and occasionally the tip of Florida. Those that nest build a platform of twigs and mosses high in a tree, usually within sight of the water.

White-Tailed Kite
Elanus leucurus
Length 15″ to 17″; Wingspread 40″

The wing span of the white-tailed kite and of the **peregrine falcon** are essentially the same. But the falcon, though rare too, still flashes across the entire continent, preying on small birds as it goes. It rarely soars, and hovers on its slim pointed wings only long enough to take aim before swooping at terrific speed, using its clenched talons to strike its feathered victim out of the air with a single blow. At a more leisurely pace, the peregrine follows the crippled bird down to feast. Seldom does it take prey any larger than a pigeon, which makes the common name of "duck hawk" for the peregrine a questionable one. For a nest site the falcon seeks seclusion, raising its young atop a tall hollow tree or on some inaccessible ledge. This is the favorite hawk of the falconer, who calls the male a "tercel," recalling the old superstition that, of the three to four eggs, only the third to be laid, produced a male chick.

Peregrine Falcon
Falco peregrinus
Length 15″ to 20″; Wingspread 40″ to 45″

North American Birds

In the depths of the swamp, **barred owls** soar with a wing span as great as 50 inches. If they cannot find a tree hole large enough to accommodate their family, they will rebuild the abandoned nest of a hawk or crow to suit their own needs. This earless owl goes forth in darkness to catch mice and other rodents, but often comes home with insects, crayfishes, frogs, and even smaller owls as its trophies of the night. East of the Rockies all the way from the Gulf of Mexico to the Atlantic shoreline and well north in Canada, the barred owl finds no need to migrate. Matching the greater food supply in southern swamps and river bottoms, it is more numerous in this portion of its range. Southerners claim that its eight-note call asks, *"Who COOKS for YOU? Who COOKS for YOU-all?"*

Barred Owl
Strix varia
Length 18" to 22"

Swamp, Stream, And Lake

Each size of tree hole matches the needs of certain kinds of birds. But failing to find one of the right dimensions near water, the common merganser and the bufflehead will nest on the ground. A four-inch hole will be enough for a bufflehead or a wood duck, which weigh only a pound or slightly more. The merganser or one of the goldeneyes—Barrow's goldeneye in the West and the common goldeneye in the East—needs a six-inch doorway, preferably wider than high. As soon as the ducklings have hatched, their parent flies to the ground and calls to them. One after another the hatchlings appear in the doorway, look out at the unfamiliar world, and launch themselves into the air. Each little body weighs less than an ounce and is covered with down only—there are no flight feathers on the fluttering wings. But with luck the ducklings land unharmed and follow, waddling in single file, as their mother leads the way to the nearest water.

The **common merganser** is a fresh-water fisherman with a long slender beak that is serrated along the sides, giving a better grip.

Common Merganser
Mergus merganser
Length 24″; Wingspread 36″

North American Birds

The bird dives for its favorite prey and finds suitable territory down the Pacific coast from Alaska to California, eastward to Newfoundland and Virginia. For winter, it flies south but seldom as far as Mexico or the Gulf States. The **bufflehead** is a diver too, but is unusual in being able to take flight with no preparatory run along the water surface. Its nesting territory is mostly west of Hudson Bay.

Bufflehead
Bucephala albeola
Length 13″ to 15½″; Wingspread 22½″

Swamp, Stream, And Lake

In winter it becomes more sociable, flocking on tidewater as well as open lakes and rivers in coastal British Columbia and in all but the north central United States.

Wood ducks can compete on equal terms with the Asiatic harlequins as the most beautiful ducks in the world. They are unique in wearing a crest that suggests a slicked-back hairdo. Mostly their diet is vegetable material, from duckweed to hard seeds. When disturbed, they rise from the water like rockets and take off through the trees, dodging agilely on a zigzag course that soon takes them out of sight and danger.

Wood Duck
Aix sponsa
Length 18"; Wingspread 28"

The goldeneyes are heavy-bodied diving ducks that swim under water while feeding on crustaceans and insects. After pattering along the water surface to get airborne, they speed up and fly faster than ducks of most other kinds. The common goldeneye nests across the northlands from Alaska to Labrador, wintering along the Pacific, Atlantic, Gulf, and Great Lakes shores as well as on rivers and smaller lakes that stay ice-free inland in most of the United States. **Barrow's goldeneye** is common in the West, but is seen in the winter along the east coast because one population in southern Greenland comes to offshore waters of the Maritime Provinces of Canada and of New England when sea ice forms farther north.

Along the Mexican border from California to Texas, two different ducks from the Tropics and South America are known as tree ducks, although only one of them nests in tree holes or often perches above the ground. They are strangely long-necked long-legged birds with high-pitched peeping notes, sounding more like young birds than adults. Peter Scott, who has studied waterfowl so extensively and raised most kinds from over the whole world, prefers to call them whistling ducks. The **black-bellied** (or red-billed) **tree ducks,** to use their official name in America, are particularly handsome with pink feet, white areas on the wings, brown backs, gray cheeks, and black underneath. The beak of the male is mostly red, grading to yellow and to blue at the tip. Failing to find a tree hole big enough, the black-bellieds will build a satisfactory nest in a fork of a high strong branch.

The **fulvous tree ducks** nest in marshy fields, flying or walking to the water. But, like other tree ducks, they prefer to wade rather than swim. They find seeds and small invertebrate animals as food in the shallows, or wander off among the sedges and grassy banks to seek additional seeds and insects. This way of life proves to be enormously versatile and successful, for fulvous tree ducks have a wider distribution than most kinds of birds: from the southwestern United States to central Mexico, and from northern South America to Argentina; in East Africa, Madagascar, India, Ceylon, and Burma.

Near water, a tree hole need not go to waste merely because it is too small for any duck or owl. **Prothonotary warblers** are always seeking nest sites in such places along streams and in swamp country

Barrow's Goldeneye
Bucephala islandica
Length 16½″ to 20″; Wingspread 28½″

Black-Bellied Tree Duck
Dendrocygna autumnalis
Length 20″ to 22″; Wingspread 37″

Fulvous Tree Duck
Dendrocygna bicolor
Length 18″ to 21″; Wingspread 36″

North American Birds

of the southeastern United States. The size of the hole is not especially critical, for these little golden-colored birds fill whatever they find with a bulky nest of plant fibers. That other larger birds have used the nest hole previously does not matter either. Both sexes of the warbler work on construction, but the female incubates alone. Somehow she keeps her mate bound to her and shows him their young when the eggs hatch. With his help, she may lead from the tree hole two broods of seven youngsters each during a single summer.

No matter how much a warbler or a wren chooses to nest near water, it remains a land bird. A kingfisher or a swallow is a land bird too, but fresh water provides the food it needs for itself and its young. The **belted kingfisher** perches on a bare branch or a telephone wire where it can look down into shallow water. It may hover to take better aim or just plunge headlong, with wings folded back, to seize its prey. Yet when it flutters into the air again with a fish held crosswise in its long sharp beak, its blue crest appears just as dry as ever. The female belted kingfisher wears an extra belt of reddish-brown across her belly below the blue chest band that marks both sexes. She is the one that does most of the digging in preparing a horizontal tunnel six to ten feet long into a steep sandy soil of a river bank. At the inner end of the tunnel she makes a nest chamber to hold her almost spherical white eggs. After the breeding season the birds fly south, some of them to marshes and waterways draining into the Gulf of Mexico and the Caribbean Sea.

Prothonotary Warbler
Protonotaria citrea
Length 5½"

Belted Kingfisher
Megaceryle alcyon
Length 11″ to 14″

The **bank swallows** that seek similar cliffs along the river wear a black belt too. Whole colonies burrow into banks, even into the sides of gravel pits, making tunnels as much as fifteen feet long and two inches in diameter, enlarged at the inner end to perhaps five inches across. From this location the parents go forth to fly low over the water, catching mayflies and caddisflies, stoneflies and gnats. Often the bank swallows pick up small weevils and other insects that fall onto the water's surface. Ranging in summer over most of North America, and also the temperate parts of Eurasia, bank swallows migrate for the winter through Mexico to South America, and to similar latitudes in the Southern Hemisphere of the Old World.

Farther up the tributary streams, where trees provide some shade, is the favored habitat of the phoebes—small flycatchers that wag their tails downward while they perch on a bare branch watching for an insect to fly near. East of the Rocky Mountains, the eastern phoebe often builds its mud nest in a sheltered crevice on the side of a gorge, or under a bridge where the nestlings are protected from rain and sun. A covering of moss may be added to conceal the bulky nest and the eggs or hungry young birds it soon contains. In the far Southwest, the black phoebe seeks similar sites, but will settle for a quiet corner of a porch or open building, particularly if it is near an irrigation ditch or a frequently watered lawn. Then the phoebe darts to the ground to pick up any insect or worm that moves. Often it carries beetles to its perch and batters them until they are mashed enough to swallow or give to the young. Both sexes feed the nestlings until they are able to fly. Then the male parent usually takes over the task of teaching the young birds to catch their own food, while his mate lays another clutch of eggs in the same nest. With this division of labor, they can often produce two or three broods in a single summer.

Of all the land birds that get their living from fresh water and build their nests beside it, none does so more consistently than the dipper or water ouzel. It frequents the mountain torrents from Panama to north central Alaska, walking boldly into the water and feasting on caddisworms, immature stoneflies, other aquatic insects, snails, and the eggs of fast-water fishes. "Find a fall, or cascade, or rushing rapid, anywhere upon a clear stream," John Muir urged, "and there you will surely find its complementary Ouzel, flitting

Bank Swallow
Riparia riparia
Length 5″ to 5½″

about in the spray, diving in foaming eddies, whirling like a leaf among beaten foam-bells; ever vigorous and enthusiastic, yet self-contained, and neither seeking nor shunning your company." Sometimes the female dipper hides her bulky oven-shaped nest under the liquid curtain of a waterfall. More often, she builds it on a rock in mid stream, or on a ledge above a noisy rapids. Skilfully she weaves its walls and roof of plant fibers and bits of soft moss, which may continue growing and stay green in the spray from the nearest cascade.

Many a time the sweet song of a dipper has been obliterated from our ears by the roar of a waterfall. By contrast, a **common loon** on its nest is always beside silent deep water. The bird cannot go farther ashore because of its body build, with legs arising close to the short tail. Unable to rise upright like a penguin, the loon can scarcely stand or take a step. But, buoyed up by water, it is an expert at diving

Common Loon
Gavia immer
Length 28" to 34"; Wingspread 54" to 58"

deep in pursuit of fishes, at swimming concealed and surfacing a half mile distant, and pattering furiously over the water until its beating wings can make its heavy body airborne. From land it cannot take off at all.

The common loon is almost synonymous with the remote lakes and rivers of northern New England and of Canada coast to coast, far into the Arctic. It is there that the loon's laugh-like calls echo from shore to shore, often at night. In winter these birds fly vigorously to the coasts and the open waters of the Great Lakes, generally traveling high and silently, with beak straight ahead and black webbed feet extending beyond the tail, straight astern.

In these days of shrinking privacy and degraded rivers, the dipper and the loon have come to symbolize the unspoiled fresh waters and a wilderness unchanged by human intruders.

CHAPTER NINE

SHORE AND OFFSHORE

As an environment, the ocean holds many special lures—its vast continuity in time and space, its hospitality to life while fresh waters ice over, its mysterious currents at many depths, and its constant renewal from the rivers of the world. Yet every bird that takes up the advantages of the open sea must forsake them when about to reproduce; for every seabird, the land is actually home.

The flying population of the ocean becomes evident each year as the birds come in succession to its shores, each kind at a special season. They seek its jutting headlands, its eroding islands, its sandy beaches and tidal gutters, its salt marshes and mangrove swamps, and the brackish estuaries.

The runoff from the land returns the water evaporated from the seas, along with a percentage of dissolved minerals—fertilizer for the coastal plant life. These important compounds come to the surface even more reliably where the contours of the bottom deflect ocean currents and cause upwelling of deep waters, rich in substances that have sunk far beyond reach of the sun. On these mineral nutrients, plankton and seaweeds grow prolifically, reproducing themselves and sustaining countless small animals and in turn, fishes and squids and seabirds.

North American Birds

So great is the variety of salt water birds that their interactions necessarily follow complex patterns. The coordination we detect in their traffic arises through a long history of continuous adjustments. Certain birds depart in springtime to nest near fresh water, or on grasslands or arctic tundras or mountain slopes. Others take their places along the coasts, without encountering competition. Some come to nest near the sea; they and their young of the year are gone before the inland migrants return.

Most exotic of the dark seabirds along American coasts are the petrels and shearwaters from the Southern Hemisphere. They visit regularly during our summer months while progressing at their own leisurely pace along migratory routes of impressive dimensions. Near New England and north to Labrador, these birds that flutter over the cold waters are of robin size—a kind of Mother Carey's chicken. Known properly as Wilson's petrels, their scientific name of *Oceanites oceanicus* emphasizes fully their marine existence. Feeding on small drifting animals among the surface plankton and on refuse dumped from ships, Wilson's petrels never stay. They return to nest on the antarctic coast and subantarctic islands. **Sooty shearwaters,** which catch fish and squid along the Pacific side of our continent in spring and fall, come from almost as far. Their home islands are Tasmania and smaller bits of land near New Zealand and the southern tip of South America. As they flap their wings and then soar up and down over the wave crests, it is hard to estimate their size, actually almost three times in body length and wing span the dimensions of a Wilson's petrel.

In summer along our southern coasts, the **magnificent frigatebirds** glide and soar as vagrants from the Tropics. On wings as much as 7½ feet tip to tip, they seem to hang in the sky, stalling their forward motion by spreading the two points of their deep-cleft tails. If a flying fish should break the water below and start on its long glide, the scissor tail snaps shut, the broad wings half close, and the bird plummets toward the sea in a straight silent dive. Just above the waves, the frigatebird spreads its wings, gapes its hooked beak, and snatches the fish, soaring back into the sky with its prey. At other times, the frigatebird earns its alternative name of "man-of-war bird" by dashing headlong at a gull, booby, or tropicbird that has caught a fish. The frigatebird takes the prey from the smaller bird and soars off with it.

Magnificent Frigatebird
Fregate magnificens
Length 37½″ to 41″; Wingspread 90″

Sooty Shearwater
Puffinus griseus
Length 16″ to 18″; Wingspread 42″

Piracy of this kind used to be commoner along the coasts, lake shores, and large rivers of North America a few decades ago, when bald eagles as the aggressors and ospreys ("fish hawks") as the victims were both more numerous. Now that both these birds of prey have grown scarce, we seldom witness the dramatic chase, the harrying of the smaller bird by one twice its weight, until the fish is transferred and the osprey turns away from the eagle to catch another meal. Only in human eyes is there a moral side to such plundering. The lives of the two unequal antagonists became adjusted long ago to allow for the aggressive interaction.

We have far more reason to wonder about the long-range effects in the balance of nature that must follow the sharp decrease in numbers of eagles, ospreys, peregrine falcons, and other predatory birds. The vacant nest sites near salt water and fresh correspond to prey that went uncaught and which may already be multiplying, unchecked by natural controls.

Of the birds that nest near the sea, the various kinds of terns and gulls and members of the shorebird group seem most likely to be affected by the decrease in attention from winged predators. In the past, it was from their chicks that misfits and orphans were culled so regularly. Around the southeastern quadrant of the continental coastline, this liberation from a beneficial hazard must influence the gull-billed tern, the whitest and one of the smallest of these birds, a resident also of Eurasian, African, and Australian shores.

Already the nesting populations of the big crested **Caspian tern** are widely scattered along the coasts of California, Newfoundland, and the north shore of the Gulf of St. Lawrence. It may be a dwindling species, although both inland and along salt water the Caspian is sometimes almost as abundant as the smaller common tern, whose nesting territories near the sea are also discontinuous. The common raises its families on the Texas coast, the Dry Tortugas islands off the tip of Florida, and up the Atlantic shoreline to Labrador.

At least four kinds of gulls that nest near the ocean have less need than ever before to guard their chicks from eagles, ospreys, and peregrine falcons. The herring gulls have already grown especially abundant along the coasts from Virginia to Greenland, and south along the Pacific Ocean to Vancouver Island. Like the much smaller laughing gulls that are seldom found far inland, they get much of

Caspian Tern
Hydroprogne caspia
Length 19″ to 23″; Wingspread 50″ to 55″

Great Black-Backed Gull
Larus marinus
Length 29″; Wingspread 65″

Shore And Offshore

their food from plowed fields. Laughing gulls nest from Nova Scotia to the West Indies and northern South America, as well as along Pacific shores of southern California and western Mexico. The **great black-backed gull** of the North Atlantic's coasts and the little **Heermann's gull,** which nests along Mexico's western shoreline before spreading northward as far as Oregon, now risk more from other predators.

The shorebirds generally rely upon protective coloration to save their eggs and chicks from direct attack. Adult oystercatchers generally hide too, among the coastal rocks or dunes, except when the ebbing tide is halfway out by day. Then they are busy on the beach, using their long red chisel-like beaks to force open the shells of bivalves, or free clinging limpets from a wet boulder, or dig in the sand for crustaceans that can be swallowed whole. The **black oystercatcher** exploits these resources from the sea northward from Baja

Heermann's Gull
Larus heermanni
Length 18″ to 21″

Black Oystercatcher
Haematopus bachmani
Length 17″ to 17½″

American Oystercatcher
Haematopus palliatus
Length 17″ to 21″

California to Alaska, while the **American oystercatcher,** which has white feathers below and on its wings, continues these operations from Baja California to Chile and along the Atlantic coast from Argentina to New Jersey. They are wary birds, incubating their eggs on bare sand in little depressions surrounded by plants too low to obscure the view in any direction.

The eastern **willets** are coastal birds whose nests in the dunes and knolls of salt marshes can be found by anyone patient enough to wait until the scolding adult has quieted down and gone straight back home. Most predators are not patient enough, which explains why willets were numerous in the East—as they still are in the inland West—until coastal settlers began robbing their nests of eggs. Today, with legal protection, these birds are regaining their former numbers and distribution, and people are a hazard mostly during the winter while the willets are hunting for food and shelter around the Gulf of Mexico south of the Texas border.

Willet
Catoptrophorus semipalmatus
Length 14″ to 17″

Semipalmated Plover
Charadrius semipalmatus
Length 6½″ to 8″

Shore And Offshore

Our smallest plovers make hardly any nest at all, but their spotted eggs and freckled downy chicks blend so well with the open beach as to be almost invisible. The **semipalmated plover** nests along Arctic coasts and as far south as British Columbia and Nova Scotia; the bird is named for the small webs between its toes, webs lacking in the piping plover and the snowy plover. The semipalmated winters from South Carolinian and southern Californian coasts to southern South America. Piping plovers, with a narrower neck band which has a broad gap in the middle on the adult female, work the upper, drier sands of the beach for insects and lay their four eggs there. Along the sea coasts they range southward to Virginia in summer, but spend the cold months on shores from South Carolina to Texas. We find **snowy plovers,** which have only the least indication of a dark collar or a black brow mark, nesting on salt flats in the West and on gravelly shores of the Gulf of Mexico. Unlike the semipalmated and the piping plovers, the snowies lay only two to three eggs. Only

Snowy Plover
Charadrius alexandrinus
Length 6″ to 7″

by accident or the most patient stalking can they ever be discovered among the pebbles. Predators do no better, which lets the snowy plover families migrate in numbers to northern South America. Actually, they are also widespread in Peru and Chile, Africa, Eurasia, and Australia.

We never tire of studying the black-necked stilts, whose red legs seem twice as long as any bird should need. They seem to skate along as they wade in water halfway to their white underparts. Nesting in marshlands far inland as well as along the coasts, they build a cup of muddy leaves and twigs, often perilously close to water level. Stilts feed almost equally on insects and small animals they can catch in marshy shallows, and range widely from southern Saskatchewan to the southern coast of Oregon, south to Peru, and from South Carolina to Brazil.

A strong wind that drives crashing waves ashore or a particularly heavy rain can endanger the nests of rails hidden in inland and coastal marshes, and of black skimmers on an open shore. The **clapper rail** builds just inches above normal high tide, favoring the tangle of grasses and reeds near tidal gutters. For two weeks both parents incubate their eggs, unable to move them, before they can lead their hatchlings from any danger. Formerly the clappers found an abundance of opportunities along both coasts of the United States, southward from northern California to Peru, and from Connecticut to Brazil. Now many of their salt marshes in the United States have been drained, and the remaining ones are poisoned frequently in attempts to reduce the number of saltmarsh mosquitoes. The Virginia rails escape some of these hazards by nesting farther north along both the Atlantic and Pacific shores, and across the mid section of the continent in fresh-water marshes of Canada and adjacent states.

Female **black skimmers** use their white breasts to prepare a hollow in the sand or pebbles of a sea beach. In it they lay their four dark brown eggs and attend to incubation while the mated males stand close by. We found one big colony of these birds making themselves at home on a disused parking lot of the Dow Chemical Company in Freeport, Texas. Eggs were everywhere. Young chicks stayed motionless while older ones ran under the shelter of bushes as we approached. Meanwhile the parents flew back and forth, their long wings almost touching the gravel, their voices sounding like barking

Black Skimmer
Rynchops nigra
Length 16″ to 20″; Widespread 42″ to 50″

Clapper Rail
Rallus longirostris
Length 14″ to 16½″

dogs. At such close range we could easily see the greater length of the lower half of the beak, which skimmers lower into the water when they cruise along to feed. Each bird leaves a wake behind it that ends abruptly when the beak touches a small fish. Instantly the skimmer bends its head down and snaps, seizing whatever it has found. Later a parent can regurgitate some of this food for its chicks, which must wait ashore and survive as best they can.

The larger wading birds—with their long legs, long necks, and long beaks—seem less subject to attack by predators and better able to adjust to changes in their wetland environment. Given a reasonable amount of protection, their numbers increase to the limit imposed by their food supply and vagaries of the weather. Around the Gulf coast from Florida to Texas, the **roseate spoonbill** nest colonially in dense clumps of red mangrove. But once their eggs have hatched, the parents are likely to leave their young unprotected during the day while going off to feed. Wading in salty shallows, the adults swing their strange beaks from side to side in an almost 180-degree arc, the spatulate tip feeling for small fishes and crustaceans which the bird can seize without looking. A spoonbill chick is fairly easy prey for a peregrine falcon or a frigatebird or even a hungry gull skimmering over the mangrove swamp.

These particular winged predators seem less likely to attack if the spoonbills have nested close to a rookery of white ibis, or of common egrets and snowy egrets that have chosen to nest near salt water instead of in a freshwater swamp. The ibises and egrets do not all desert the young at once and, if danger appears, those adults that have remained behind fly up and back and forth. This umbrella of white wings and bodies moving in every possible direction above the nest area discourages some birds of prey, but rarely stops a crow or a flock of great-tailed grackles from darting in and gorging themselves. This largest of the grackles, known formerly as the boat-tailed grackle, generally nests near by among the salt-marsh vegetation. Its mixed diet of animal and plant foods is available all year through most of its range around shores of the Gulf of Mexico and north along the Atlantic Ocean as far as New Jersey. From Louisiana westward into Mexican waters, it also attacks the eggs and young chicks of the white-faced ibis.

Roseate Spoonbill
Ajaia ajaia
Length 33″; Wingspread 52″

Brown Pelican
Pelecanus occidentalis
Length 50″; Wingspread 80″

The ibises and egrets never dive for fish. Green herons often do. **Brown pelicans,** which are the state birds of Louisiana, make a practice of getting food by plunging from as much as 70 feet above the water. Yet these are matters of custom and not body build, for the white pelicans put no more than their heads and necks below the surface to reach the prey they want.

Brown pelicans fly in long lines, alternately flapping and coasting, just above the water. Their nesting territory extends along Pacific shorelines from Vancouver Island to Chile, and from South Carolina to the West Indies, around the Gulf of Mexico and the Caribbean Sea to the Guianas. Unlike white pelicans, they often nest in shrubs and trees, where the young birds must wait an extra month to leave home—until their flight feathers grow out. Pelicans that hatch in nests upon the ground can waddle off to explore their world in five weeks instead of nine. In either situation, the youngsters have their food brought to them. At first their meals are a regurgitated fish soup, served in their parents' pouches. Later, as their own beaks grow longer, they reach right down an old bird's throat to take whatever is inside the crop.

Islands off the coast, particularly those with precipitous sides, give seabirds the greatest protection from nonflying predators. Wherever storm waves have hammered at a rocky shoreline and isolated rocky outcroppings, certain fish- and squid-eating birds will divide up the sanctuary. They need a minimum of space for a nest and can cope with a territory only inches across.

Brandt's cormorant breeds despite extreme crowding on jagged islands just off the California coast. Each pair has its own little saucered platform, built of a firm mixture of seaweed and excrement, like the landing on a staircase. Generally the nest site is inherited when previous occupants fail to return and claim it, or is taken by young and vigorous nesters from a pair that has grown old and feeble. The cormorants fly off from the nest and alight on it almost vertically, to escape being pecked by neighboring birds to right and left, upslope and down. Even the young birds must be masters of

Brandt's Cormorant
Phalacrocorax penicillatus
Length 33″ to 35″

North American Birds

the art of vertical take-off, for on the nest site they cannot step in any direction without invading the domain of an intolerant neighbor.

On Bonaventure Island, a few hundred yards beyond the Gaspésian coastline at Percé, Québec, one strip of land along the crest of the windy precipitous east side supports the nests of about 50,000 **gannets,** which is a third of the total North Atlantic population. To our eyes, all adult gannets appear identical. Each is perfectly

Gannet
Morus bassanus
Length 36"; Wingspread 72"

groomed, glistening white except for creamy feathers on head and neck and black giving emphasis around the eyes, wing tips, and legs. Yet each bird allows only one other—its mate of the year—to settle on the square yard of nesting space it defends. But a gannet can't even make a mistake unless the wind is strong, for it needs a good breeze to lift its body even when its wings are spread their full 70 inches. Only along the actual rim of the island can birds leap out into space and be airborne at any time. Seemingly this is why the colony is crowded together on less than six acres. Every one of the 22 gannetries in the world is organized in the same way—like a city without streets or sewers, government or police force. But neither are there riots or crimes—at least none worse than filching some seaweed nesting material from a neighbor who is taking a nap.

In a colony of **royal terns,** the population may be even denser—as many as six pairs per square yard. Automatically they swivel to face

Royal Tern
Thalasseus maximus
Length 19″; Wingspread 43″

the slightest breeze, which keeps all of the birds facing in the same direction. The heavy orange beak and black cap of one nester points directly to the white tail and crossed gray wingtips of the next one upwind. At intervals, some local disturbance excites the birds, and, as though on signal, they flash out their wings and take off. They fly around screaming harshly, only to settle again in a minute or less as though nothing had happened. Royal terns nest on small islands off the coasts of Baja California and southern California, around the Gulf of Mexico to Louisiana, and from the West Indies as far north as Maryland. In winter they fly as far south as Argentina. A separate population of these birds lives along African coasts.

So many of the seabirds of offshore islands range widely in the Arctic that we wonder which came first: the nesting on rocky outposts, or nesting close to favored food in frigid water. These sites are particularly popular among members of the family Alcidae—the auks and guillemots and puffins—which have short necks, wings, and tails on sturdy bodies. All swim readily in the sea, propelling themselves under water with their oar-like wings, steering with trailing feet. Most catch small fishes, but the **pigeon guillemots** of the North Pacific swim all the way to the bottom to feed on a great variety of worms, crustaceans, and other sea creatures. Yet for breeding purposes they seek out the same kinds of nest sites as their fish-eating kin. Sometimes the female pigeon guillemot lays her two eggs on grassy turf. At others she makes her home in a burrow, perhaps abandoned by a rabbit. She may find a saucer-shaped cranny in the wall of a sea grotto or precipitous cliff and manage fairly well to keep her eggs from falling over the edge of the narrow shelf. Pigeon guillemots nest along the ocean shores from southern California to the northern islands of Japan. Almost incredibly, these birds winter in the Arctic off the Aleutian islands, diving in almost total darkness whenever they are hungry.

The guillemots of the North Atlantic are the black guillemots which come south for the winter, prefer small fishes for food, and lack the black wedges in the white shoulder patch that distinguish their Pacific kin. We have met black guillemots near the southern end of their American breeding range, on a bleak island about 25 miles offshore from Rockland, Maine. The guillemots' share of Matinicus Rock is mostly near the lighthouse, in places where long ago storm waves have eroded narrow slots like crevasses into the granite. At the bottom of these slots the birds had gathered a trifling of plant materials to mark a nest, and laid two pointed eggs. On some the parent was still incubating. Other nests had untended pairs of chicks waiting for the next delivery of fish. About once an hour, each parent would return with its beak full of small fishes held crosswise, heads flopping on one side and tails on the other. Without dropping any, the guillemot fluttered down and fed the chicks, then beat its way out of the narrow chasm and rested a while on some high rock overlooking the open sea. It was then that the bird resembled a pigeon with almost no tail and with blood-red feet. Fishermen often call them "sea pigeons."

On the opposite side of this little island, which has an area of only a few acres, common puffins tended their obese young in crannies below huge boulders storm waves had not yet swept away. The mated parents came and went without delay or ceremony, feeding their chicks in the dark seclusion. Two- and three-year-old puffins perched along the windward cliff, or fluttered down to the waves to dive for their next meal. These puffins were still too young to breed, but already had the urge to become familiar with the island. Probably they had been hatched there. Puffin chicks are stuffed by their

Pigeon Guillemot
Cepphus columba
Length 12″ to 14″

parents until they reach a critical stage in development, and are then left to starve. In solitude they slim down, feather out, and start off on their own some night—into the open, over to the cliff edge—and crash-dive to the sea below. They must learn to fish, to fly, and to find their way back in a later year to an island of similar sort. By then their wide, short beaks of chickhood have grown colorful covers whose stripes are a progressive record of age.

Exposed parts of Matinicus Rock attract seabirds that nest in colonies: great black-backed gulls on the highest largest promontory; herring gulls slightly lower and nearer the middle of the island; laughing gulls still lower near the opposite end; and arctic terns on the bare bald summit around the lighthouse. Clumps of eider down among the rounded rocks between the herring-gull colony and the sea showed that the island's gentlest slope had been used by the same mother eider ducks that still floated and dove with their ducklings in shallow water.

One more—an eighth—kind of seabird hid in fair numbers on the island. Wherever the island had soil a few inches deep, Leach's petrels had come at night using their feet and beaks to dig out their nesting burrows. In darkness they came and went, avoiding the hungry gulls, finding their individual holes in the shallow turf. Usually an adult that had been gathering food at sea for about eighteen hours entered to twitter and trill a greeting to its mate. It would spend the next 30 hours on guard; before dawn the mate would have left on a similar mission, to return the next night after dark. Two adults are in the burrow at midnight, and one is still there through the daylight hours. There is no sign of their chick until it is ready to hover with forked tail spread, to fish from the sea surface, and to wander over the open ocean. In the Atlantic, Leach's petrels nest on islands off Cape Cod, Massachusetts, to Labrador and Iceland; in winter they spread southward beyond the Equator. Those of Pacific waters breed from Baja California to Korea, sometimes wandering to Hawaii and the Galápagos Islands but usually wintering well north toward Bering Strait.

Of all the seabirds, the most bizarre may well be the **tufted puffin** nesting on coasts and islands around the North Pacific from southern California to Japan. In breeding season an adult is basically black, not counting two red feet, an oversize beak cover striped with red

Tufted Puffin
Lunda cirrhata
Length 14⅓″ to 15½″

and yellow, a white face that appears to have been painted on, and tufts of golden feathers arching backward from behind the eyes like the makeup of a clown. Each pair raises its single chick in a burrow dug into the turf sloping toward the sea or, if crowded out, on a ledge or in a rock crevice equally close to the open water. In autumn, the golden plumes and the beak cover are shed. The winter plumage comes in dark over the head, back, and wings, and in brownish-gray spreads below. But a new beak cover starts to grow with an extra ridge and an added band of color. Gradually the adornment of mating time develops, and the birds return from their offshore winter fishing grounds to raise another generation.

For anyone interested in birds, the sea coast is never a disappointment at any time of year. As soon as the many nesters and their young move out, others arrive to make use of the same resources. More kinds may be present in the winter months than during the breeding season, for they fly to the sea beaches and salt marshes and estuaries from most of the northern, inland area of the continent. They come from the mountains, from the tundras, from the grasslands and other homes near fresh waters that freeze over. Sometimes the edge of the ocean suggests the footlight boundary of a great stage, on which all the actors playing their parts during the year come on for a mass curtain call.

From the high mountains and the High Arctic the water pipits come, and wag their tails as they walk over the muddy shores. Along Pacific coasts the surfbirds spread out, southward to the Tropics from their homeland in Alaska. Each has taken on a gray chest coloration that obscures the pattern of spots marking the bird's whole underside in summer. The crown and back are darker too, but the black triangle still shows at the tail tip in flight and the legs are just as lemon-yellow.

From the grasslands, both shorebirds and characteristic gulls arrive. The **long-billed curlews** whir and soar, flying long distances at night until they reach their destinations in the Southwest, including shores of California, Mexico, and Texas. Still they probe the beach and cry *KUR-LEW*. Marbled godwits cross the Central flyway to reach the same Pacific shores, or follow the Atlantic coast to Florida and the Gulf of Mexico. Black-headed Franklin's gulls get a gray cap, a white face and throat, and leave the prairies by the Central

Long-Billed Curlew
Numenius americanus
Length 20″ to 26″

North American Birds

flyway for the Gulf coasts of Louisiana and Texas and the Pacific shores of Guatemala south to Ecuador. California gulls leave their admirers inland and wing their way to Pacific waters from Vancouver Island southward.

As though flying against the wintering stream, the **black petrels** that raised their young in underground seclusion on islands along Baja California wander northward along the California coast, as well as southward to waters off Peru.

Black Petrel
Loomelania melania
Length 9″

The biggest contingents come from the arctic tundras, streaming toward the ice-free ocean margins, the Gulf of Mexico, and estuarine waters. The arctic loons head for the Pacific coast from Alaska south, the red-throated loons for both sides of the cooling continent. The gull-like fulmars shift their scavenging well offshore, ranging south over the Pacific to the Mexican boundary, but in the Atlantic only to the edge of the winter ice.

Great flocks of blue geese take the Mississippi flyway from around Hudson Bay to the Gulf coast, while the more widespread snow geese —their closest kin—travel all the flyways to reach salt marshes where food will continue to meet their needs until spring. The black brant from shallows of the Arctic Ocean and coastal Alaska move southwest to warmer bays down the Pacific shoreline. In winter plumage they have largely lost the distinctively complete white collar by which they can be recognized from the ordinary brant, whose throat is black. The ordinary brant, however, show allegiance to Atlantic waters by migrating southeast to spend the cold months along the eastern coast. White-fronted geese choose either the Pacific or the central flyways, following them to marshlands of the Pacific states and Texas.

The little harlequin ducks spread east and west, staying in small groups by themselves or sharing the saltwater shallows with surf scoters from across the polar tundras. The common eiders can find the shellfish and crustaceans they eat without going so far; they socialize in great flotillas off the coasts as far south as northern British Columbia and Chesapeake Bay. Oldsquaws seek the same kinds of food, but reach them without much competition by moving farther offshore where the water is as much as 200 feet deep, and by continuing farther south—to the coasts of Washington state and to South Carolina. Red-breasted mergansers catch their favorite fishes more reliably by migrating still nearer the Tropics, reaching Baja California on one side of the continent and Florida on the other.

Shorebirds have changed to winter plumage by the time they come from the tundras to saltwater shorelines. The black-bellied plovers are no longer black-bellied, although they still retain their identifying black marks between their bodies and the under side of their wings. They migrate over most of the continent to east, west, and

Gulf coasts; many of them continue on to southern Brazil and Chile. Whimbrels follow the Pacific and Atlantic flyways to these same destinations.

From Alaskan nesting grounds the long-billed dowitchers head for the coast of California, and the Gulf of Mexico from Florida to Guatemala. They mingle with short-billed dowitchers from tundras east and west of Hudson Bay, as well as birds from Alaska. Both have lost the brown from their plumage and appear mostly gray—darker on wings and back and cap, and pale mist color underneath. As though the long-billeds had farther to go, they start out in late summer for their southward flights, calling *DOWITCH* to one another as they go. Similarly, the lesser yellowlegs precedes the greater yellowlegs, down the latitudes as soon as the young of the year can fly well, and back to the nesting grounds at the first hint of spring.

Black turnstones have exchanged their spotted black-and-white feathers on neck and sides for more uniform grayish-brown before moving southward along the Pacific coast as far as northern Mexico. Though they travel the westernmost flyway with the ruddy turnstones from Alaskan breeding grounds, the blacks settle for the winter while the ruddies keep going, some to remote islands in the South Pacific. The ruddies are no longer ruddy, although their black markings still show on their chests and sides. Their heads and necks have lost the white feathers and turned gray-brown like the back and wings. These changes affect the more eastern populations too, as the ruddy turnstones take the Mississippi and Atlantic flyways to South Carolina, the Gulf coast, and on to southern Brazil.

Southbound sanderlings are paler too, but they scamper along the beach and follow the receding waves with no change of pace. Their total numbers must be incredibly great, for there are plenty of sanderlings to delight the beachcomber in winter from British Columbia south on Pacific shores and from Massachusetts to Florida and around the Gulf, with still more on virtually every sandy margin of salt water to the tip of South America. In winter, sanderlings are "whiteys," and conspicuously bigger and faster than the semipalmated and least sandpipers with which they often flock. Western sandpipers from Alaska, wintering from California and North Carolina southward, wade out where the water is calm and probe the bottom even by submerging their whole heads. Sometimes the dunlins join the smaller sandpipers, each dunlin grayer for the winter and without the black belly marking that is so distinct in breeding season.

Generally we see no northern phalarope, or dovekie, or parasitic jaeger along the shores of temperate latitudes unless a winter storm has driven the bird to land from the open seas. At this season the phalaropes resemble sanderlings, but have a few pale lines along the back and a black mark through each eye. The little dovekies, with their short beaks and compact bodies, act bewildered; in their winter plumage they have white throats and white along each side of the head toward the black nape. The jaegers may be the most confused of all for during the storm they have lost sight of the terns they were following over the ocean to get fish the easy, parasitic way.

Sometimes we wish these seasonal visitors from the tundras wore some kind of colorful marker that would help us tell them apart from the winter birds from freshwater breeding grounds. But the birds arrive with no help from travel agents and no emblems to keep a tour group together. Each flier has its own directions hidden in its genetic heritage, a chemical Baedeker with an answer for every normal circumstance.

At the approach and end of winter, the black terns flit along both ocean coasts but never stay. Their passage is a signal that the other migrants from freshwater margins will be responding to the change of seasons too. The spotted sandpipers will arrive, without their spots but still with their habit of fluttering along like dragonflies with stiff wings and diving into the water to snatch a crustacean before it gets away. The big western grebes will head west. Horned grebes, half the size of the westerns but now like them white on neck and cheeks, divide their total population—some to the Pacific coast, others down the Mississippi flyway to the Gulf of Mexico, and still others along the Atlantic shoreline.

This winter realignment, from fresh waters to the sea coasts, is so general a pattern in North America that any exceptions require explanation. The double-crested cormorants migrate in V formations east, west, and south to salt shallows where they can continue to dive from the surface and swim after fish while completely submerged. We know them from common loons with the same habit by their hooked beaks, shorter necks, and longer tails. But the loons never need to stand out on shore afterward to dry their feathers the way cormorants all do.

Canada geese use all the flyways, but tend to be clannish. Apparently this accounts for the existence of at least ten distinct populations, differing slightly in color pattern and considerably in size. The smallest, called cackling geese, weigh no more than five pounds; they breed in Alaska and winter in the central valley of California, never joining the flocks of somewhat larger Canada geese in salt marshes along the Pacific coast. The giants, for many years believed extinct, are still rare, nesting only in the north central United States and following the central flyway to secluded marshes along the Gulf; some of these birds weigh eighteen pounds.

Of all the ducks that dabble and tip in freshwater shallows, the pintails are the most widely distributed in summer. For winter vast numbers of them move to the coasts, continuing their feeding along edges of the saltmarsh channels. At the slightest disturbance every one in a flock flashes its slender pointed wings and rises almost straight up before choosing a direction for a fast getaway. By contrast, of the ducks that dive from the surface and swim underwater to get a larger proportion of animal food, all but the buffleheads have heavier bodies and must run along the wave tops to get airborne. The redheads and lesser scaups often join forces, forming great flotillas including hundreds of individuals. The canvasbacks usually stay separate and in saltier water; we recognize them by their paler backs and flat foreheads, noticeable even in silhouette.

The goldeneyes seem somehow special, and often follow a daily routine for the winter months. As the light fades in the afternoon, they fly far off the coast and stay there in flocks until dawn brightens the sky. Then they return to dive for crabs and mollusks in deeper water than most of the bay ducks. The two populations of Barrow's goldeneye stay separate, the one from Greenland and northern Labrador moving south as far as Long Island Sound. Those from Alaska and interior British Columbia use the Pacific flyway as far as northern California. But a good many manage not to migrate at all because they have found fresh waters that stay open all year, thanks to thermal springs, such as those on Lake Yellowstone, Wyoming.

This kind of sanctuary, sustained by earth's inner heat, also accounts for the presence of nonmigratory trumpeter swans in Wyoming and adjacent parts of Montana and Idaho. The only migratory trumpeters left are in the Far Northwest, and winter along the coast of southern Alaska and British Columbia. Trumpeters with the inherited directions for coming to the Atlantic coast and the broad waters of the Mississippi Delta were exterminated before Audubon had a chance to paint them.

Sometimes we wonder whether the white pelicans ever wintered along Atlantic shores before anyone thought to mark it down. They still come southwest to Pacific waters and the Gulf of California, and from the southwest corner of Florida around the Gulf of Mexico. In all these places they wade in the shallows, often sociably, and herd the small fishes into a *cul-de-sac*. At each scoop of its beak, a white pelican can then catch dozens of its favorite food.

When a pelican swims, it floats higher in the water than a swan and conceals all the black feathers of its wing tips. But buoyant as the pelican is, its long beak and pouch are too heavy to be extended ahead when it flies. Instead, it folds its neck in the shape of a Z, spreads its great wings, and kicks itself into the air kangaroo-fashion, with both webbed feet at once. With tremendous flapping and ungainly hops it gets under way. Suddenly the bird is the personification of grace and dignity, gliding along as though weightless. In migration, too, the white pelicans in formation wheel and soar at great heights, exciting our admiration as we stare up at them from the ground.

Along the southern coasts and on some of the freshwater breeding grounds of white pelicans, their swimming companions are often the common American coots. These noisy little chicken-like birds also float high, nodding their heads as they paddle around. When they come out on marshy spots of land to feed, the gray lobes on their unwebbed toes can be seen. For other delicacies, coots dive. But they get into position for swimming downward by making a comical little upward jump from the surface. To fly they rush along the water, beating their short wings furiously and kicking with both feet alternately, in the manner of diving ducks.

If people along the shore offer free food, the coots and pelicans learn to come—at least to see whether the offerings are to their liking. Grain, peanuts, and bits of fruit appeal to a coot. A fisherman can tempt a pelican with wastes from the fish he is cleaning. And soon the shore grows noisy with the cries of gulls flocking in to see what they can get. Settling on the water or taking off again, flying back and forth in all directions, the number of different kinds of gulls may seem bewildering.

Probably there are only two kinds present: the ubiquitous herring gulls, and the slightly smaller ring-billed gulls. The multiplicity of feather patterns and leg and beak colorings arises from the fact that juvenile markings are present for two age classes—young birds in their first winter and those in their second. Older birds show adult coloration.

In its first winter, a young herring gull is brown, with a dark tail, dark legs, and a black beak. A year later its tail will be broadly dark, but its body will be gray, its head streaked or spotted; its legs will be pink, and its beak getting pale. The adults have flesh-colored legs and only an orange spot near the tip of its yellow beak. That spot is important: a target for the hatchling gull to peck if it is to induce its parent to regurgitate food. Adult ring-billed gulls have a similar spot as well as the black ring for which they are named; their legs and feet are yellow. Immature ring-billed resemble herring gulls in their second winter, but have only a narrow dark band across the tail close to its white edge. In separate flocks or in a mixture of the two kinds of gulls, we cannot tell the herrings from the ring-billeds by their calls. But we feel sure the gulls can; their cries provide meaningful communication. To us they are intriguing sounds of the sea coast— more representative of it than any other.

CHAPTER TEN

WHILE THERE'S STILL TIME

THE YEAR WAS 1820 WHEN JOHN JAMES AUDUBON, BANKRUPT BUT STILL clutching a portfolio of paintings he had begun toward his *Birds of America*, left Cincinnati to travel down the Mississippi River by drifting flatboat. By 1838 his dream had come to reality; all of the illustrations had arrived from the engravers and his accompanying text, the *Ornithological Biographies*, was in print. Through his own efforts and great skills, Audubon had made himself solvent and famous, respected alike in North America and Europe.

During those same eighteen years, the human population of America north of the Rio Grande increased from about 10 to 17 million. Immigration accounted for much of this rapid change. The majority of people were farmers who, along with stockraisers, hunters, trappers, fishermen, whalers, woodsmen, and miners, earned a living for themselves while keeping the rest of the population supplied with land and water products. The producers purchased services from the urban people—including blacksmiths and harness makers, millers and sawyers, printers and preachers, tailors and teachers, bankers and clerks, barmaids and errand boys. The newspapers of those days told of the first steamboat to go up the Mississippi River and the first steamship to cross the Atlantic under its own power. Indians were still fighting the colonists for the West.

Audubon lived until 1851, seventeen years before the first coast-to-coast railroad was completed. The telegraph had just been invented, but no transoceanic cables had been built. Yet Audubon was already trying to impress upon the many he knew that America's rapid progress was being purchased at an incredible cost in terms of wildlife. Never in recorded history had so many animals been killed or deprived of shelter in so few years.

"Dead as the dodo" was a common expression in Audubon's day, even among people who could not have explained that the dodo was a flightless pigeon, native to the island of Mauritius in the Indian Ocean, where it went extinct in the 1600's. Audubon had no need for such foreign examples to realize the plight of vanishing birds. He knew that among his life-sized bird portraits he could never include one of the great auk. This flightless bird that had thronged North Atlantic coasts by the millions became extinct during Audubon's own lifetime. Formerly the goose-sized great auks nested among gannets and guillemots on small islets all around the cold North Atlantic. They swam in migration to spend the winter off shores as far south as Florida and Gibraltar. Primitive people caught great auks as food, and raided their nests for edible eggs.

The last great auks in the New World were efficiently clubbed to death about 1840 to supply feathers for feather beds, pillows, and comforters. The men who finished them off had climbed onto sea-bound islets while the birds were nesting there. The fatty bodies were scalded in big pots of boiling sea water to free the feathers, and then tossed into the fire as fuel. By 1844 the great auk was extinct, represented in all the world by only two mounted skins, a dozen skeletons, and a few blown eggs.

No one knows whether Audubon himself saw the last carbonated warblers. He shot a pair near Henderson, Kentucky, in May of 1811, and drew them immediately for Plate 60 of his *Birds of America*. His description in the *Ornithological Biographies* indicates that they were males, probably not yet in full plumage. Certainly their markings differ distinctly from those of any related birds, and it is unlikely that Audubon realized their rarity. No specimens were kept, and no one ever recorded the bird again.

Four more of the birds painted by Audubon are now extinct: the Labrador duck (1878); the passenger pigeon (1914); the Carolina paroquet (1920); and the heath hen (1933). Several others are among the 334 rare or vanishing birds of the world, including "those thought to be extinct, but of which detailed information is still lacking." This compilation was published in 1965 by the Survival Service, a committee established as a central clearing house for information gathered by member states of the International Union for the Conservation of Nature, with headquarters at Morges, Switzerland. Two of the six North American warblers listed are birds that Audubon knew —Kirtland's warbler, and Bachman's warbler—depicted by Audubon against a branch of Franklinia flowers and leaves. Franklinia trees would be extinct, too, had not the botanist who discovered one in Georgia saved a cutting and established it in his Philadelphia garden.

Counting the offshore islands as parts of the North American scene, the birds now rarest or in greatest danger are these:

Bermudian petrel	Attwater's prairie	Hudsonian godwit
Trumpeter swan	chicken	Ivory-billed
Canada goose—	Greater prairie chicken	woodpecker
Aleutian race	Whooping crane	Pribilov wren
Canada goose—	Sandhill crane—	Bachman's warbler
Giant race	Florida race	Kirtland's warbler
Everglades kite	Clapper rail—	Ipswich sparrow
California condor	Yuma race	Dusky seaside sparrow
Bald eagle—	Eskimo curlew	Cape Sable sparrow
Southern race		

Of these, the Bermudian petrel, Eskimo curlew, Hudsonian godwits, and ivory-billed woodpecker dropped out of sight for a number of years, and then turned up again in remote refuges.

A third of the endangered species have the misfortune to be large and conspicuous. They also need space, harder to find now that they must share their continent north of Mexico with nearly 325 million people. Perhaps there is reason to rejoice that almost 650 different kinds of birds can still find nesting sites in Canada, Bermuda, and the United States—not counting Hawaii, whose state bird (the gentle little néné goose) is also on the danger list. Appreciation for our wild heritage has already led to the establishment of sanctuaries and special programs of assistance that seem likely to save the trumpeter swans and the nénés from extinction and, with luck, the whooping cranes and spectacular ivory-billed woodpeckers too.

Rescuing the California condor and Kirtland's warbler seems to require measures that homeowners fear: controlled burning to get rid of underbrush and trees, maintaining the habitat these birds need to survive. The condor presents the greater challenge, since it must be able not only to see dead animals from the air but also have nest privacy in the state with our fastest growing population. The Kirtland's warbler has become, as Les Lines of the National Audubon Society writes, "the bird worth a forest fire." Today, when these warblers return from wintering in the Bahamas to seek nest sites among the young jack pines in Michigan, they have a place waiting for them where the trees are just the right size.

Saving the Everglades kite may be mostly a matter of protecting the great swamplands of southern Florida from drought, which decreases the population of snails upon which this bird feeds almost exclusively. The southern race of the bald eagle, like the Bermudian petrel and many other carnivorous birds including the osprey, is in greater peril. Their eggs and young fail to develop normally because of poisons the parent birds are getting in their food.

Even far out at sea, the Bermudian petrels are meeting small fishes and squids containing dangerous amounts of DDT and other chlorinated hydrocarbons. These inexpensive insecticides pollute the broad oceans from pole to pole, increasing slowly in concentration because they do not readily decompose. Microscopic green plants among the drifting plankton absorb the poisons. Small animals get them in the plants they eat and store them in fats (mostly for lack of a way to excrete them) but seldom live long enough to be affected themselves. Larger animals prey on the smaller and are left with the same poisons from the fats they digest. They also attain a greater average age and come to accumulate dangerous amounts.

Near the coasts, these poisons from the land reach higher concentrations in the sea. Fishes that sicken become easy prey for ospreys, and ones that are cast ashore attract eagles that have not found an osprey to rob. The parent ospreys and eagles, like the parent petrels, may tolerate the insecticides. But their reproduction suffers, and the adults become sterile. Abandoned nests and sharply lower census figures show the rate of change.

While There's Still Time

As the human population grows, so does the number of people who are determined that the birds of America shall not shrink until posterity is left with the introduced house sparrow and starling, the ubiquitous gulls, and the few others that benefit from civilization. Feathered North Americans can be a cherished heritage into the far future, a treasured facet of the out-of-doors. They provide a special kind of wealth—one that loses its value and its life if we touch it.

INDEX

335